A Good While Back

Remembering a Simpler Time

A Good While Back

Remembering a Simpler Time

OLIETA EDWARDS

JOMÁGA HOUSE

A Good While Back
Remembering a Simpler Time

ISBN-13: 978-1-60495-055-7
Copyright © 2019 by Olieta Edwards. Published in the USA by Jomága House, an imprint of The Jomága Group, LLC. All rights reserved. No part of this book may be reproduced in any form or by any electronic or mechanical means, including information storage and retrieval systems, without permission in writing, except as provided by USA Copyright law.

In Memory of Kenneth C. Edwards,

his birth family and mine.

Dedicated to family and friends, and future generations.

I hope you find pleasure in reading this book.

Thank you to my editor/publisher, Terri Kalfas,

for your diligence and patience

in working to bring a dream to completion.

Foreword

My life was so different from that of our children that it seems good to give at least a glimpse of how it was in the 1930s and the 1940s on a small farm in southern Missouri.

Things have been invented and opportunities have opened that could not have even been imagined back then. As my paternal grandmother said as she was about to turn ninety years old, "I feel like a storybook."

Although I spent only my first eighteen years in Dent County, Missouri, it was the backdrop for everything in my life since then, as it should be, for this time was the greatest time of learning.

I found so many interesting things to notice back then. The sounds, the smells, the shapes of things in the environment, as well as people, have always interested me. Maybe most notable of all were the things I appreciated without actually knowing they were much different in that setting than other things I would encounter as I am going through life.

My formative years were when "denim" meant "overalls" and were work clothes; women wore dresses; and people dressed up for church instead of dressing down. It was before jeans became almost universal as anytime wear and practically unisexual, except for being made to fit many different body types.

A Good While Back

Another Word:

Looking back (again) I realize there is something I was about to overlook: how very blessed I have actually been throughout my entire life. Though I wasn't always aware of it, there have been so many blessings in my life it is time now to acknowledge this fact: God Is Good.

Part 1

Part I

Chapter 1

It was in the time of the Great Depression. Herbert Hoover was probably a brilliant man, but as president he had not figured out ways to help the people, so he was not considered a successful president. My Mother's comment on the situation was "that old Hoover" with dislike and disdain in her voice.

Then President Franklin Delano Roosevelt came on the scene. He came in as president in 1933, the year after I was born. Times were very hard. Some folks met the challenge and managed to get by. Others didn't do so well.

I didn't know anyone who was in either the CCC (Civilian Conservation Corps) or the WPA (Works Progress Administration) but I do remember that they were sort of looked down upon. The CCC and WPA were programs instituted under Mr. Roosevelt that probably actually did some real good, in that some things were actually improved and idle hands were put to work. We could see the work of the CCC on the roads not too far away from where we lived, because we were close to the Clark National Forest where they did a lot of their work.

I don't remember feeling deprived during that time. We met the challenges and with fortitude, stick-to-it-ivness, and humor, got by fairly well. I say "we" a lot, for as part of the family I felt included.

I am Olieta Mae Russell Edwards. I was born—weighing nine pounds—at 10 o'clock one morning in early January 1932 to

A Good While Back

Myrtle Maud Springman Russell and Ray Hadley Russell. They were not unaware of the challenges before them, but they had skills and experience that would stand them in good stead through the sometimes-difficult years ahead. They were already used to hard work, sharing, and being helpful to others.

My mother was third in a family of twelve children. When she was in the eighth grade, she was needed at home to help her mother, so she left school. She would have had at least five younger siblings, and maybe six, then.

I don't remember hearing how the other children related to the situation, whether anyone else was needed that badly or not. Mom always seemed to be very sensitive to her mother's family situation. Maybe the others were, too. I never heard of any of them feeling uncared for.

Mom was the quiet one of the girls, maybe because she was the middle sister. Her older sister, Laura, was confident and outspoken and her younger sister, Hildred, was cute with curly hair.

My dad was the only boy in his family to reach adulthood. Because Granddad had been crippled by polio (as the family learned later), he depended on Dad for a lot of things when Dad was old enough to help. Dad had an older sister and two younger sisters. Grandma lost a set of boy and girl twins when they were very young, and an infant girl to pneumonia.

I am not sure at which house I was born; there was a picture, supposedly of me with another little girl on a porch, so I think maybe we lived in that house first.

It seems from the pictures of me at that time that I was a pretty baby with plenty of dark hair. My mother's uncle commented that I had so much hair I looked like a varmint. He had a granddaughter just a little older than I was who was very fair. Besides, he did have a way with words.

I once overheard the comment, "She was such a pretty baby" (sigh). Was that a comment on my then-current looks and demeanor?

Part I

The earliest home I remember was a log house. At least that was what it looked like on the inside. It had two rooms, separated by a partition that was probably in the center of the house; the door connecting them was somewhat toward the front of the house. The front door was near the center of the house on the west side of the partition, and the back door was in the center of the east-side room.

In those days the main bed was in the front room, which was a combination bedroom and living room. There were two slender windows on the west end as if flanking a fireplace, but we had a wood stove in that spot in the winter. The big feather bed was very tall and sat with the head against the inside wall. (Called a feather bed because there was a large bed-size "tick" (bag) filled with feathers placed on top of a regular bed.) There was also a stand table with turned legs and a wide rocking chair with a fake leather seat and flat wide armrests. I was told I rocked that chair so hard I turned it over backwards. I think I remember rocking in it. I also think I broke the wide center slat in the back. When things like that happened, repairs didn't always get made.

The kitchen held a cook stove at the east end of the house. In a small shelf behind the stove, sort of in a log crevice, Mom kept cod liver oil. The table sat by the window, which was on the front side of the house. By the back door a washstand held a wash pan, a hand towel and a water bucket with a dipper for drinking.

Since we had no real closets in this tiny house, a small area in the back of the kitchen was curtained off to serve that purpose. I recall an aunt once fluttering in and out of that area, fearfully, as my uncle was speaking to Dad outside the kitchen door.

In retrospect this all sounds kind of romantic and adventurous. It certainly didn't bother me. I'm sure it didn't bother Mom either. She was always one to cope and make the best of things. I think it probably had a lot to do with the fact that she married my dad knowing the responsibilities he already carried. (His dad needed help on the farm.) Mom and Dad cared very much for each other.

Out the back door and a little way from the corner of the house was a cistern from which we drew water for our household needs. This was like a really big concrete jug in the ground into which rainwater from the roof of the house was drained after first letting the rain rinse off the house.

A few things I remember from that house were: My dad and Uncle Bill drilling (quizzing) me on the word "stand" (I was about 3 years old at the time), in the front room by lamplight; Dad and Uncle Bill showing me a red toy truck that had headlights. I never saw the truck again. Maybe it was for children Uncle Bill hoped to have.

I do not remember much about my sister, Oneta, at this time. She was born November 1933. I guess she was just always around.

I do remember my paternal grandmother walking me back up the lane from their house so I could see my new baby brother. I went up to the high bed to see my brother but the bed was too tall and I couldn't see him. They named him Donald Ray for my dad. He was born April 1936.

PART I

CHAPTER 2

We had a Victrola. Mom had a piano when she got married and her sister, Laura, offered to trade the Victrola for the piano. Of course a piano would not have fit into that tiny little house, so the trade was made. Later when we would go to see Aunt Laura and her family, I had trouble keeping my hands off the piano. I wanted to try to play it so badly, but I did not want to be a problem.

When I was about three or four years old I had a little china tea set with probably four cups, four saucers, a sugar bowl, a creamer and a teapot. It was a kind of gleaming gold color with a pretty design. I played with it on Grandma Russell's concrete screened-in porch. Of course, over time I broke most of the set, but I eventually quit playing with it and saved a cup, sugar bowl with lid, and another lid.

Once, when Dad needed to go see a neighbor, Henry Riggens, about something, he took me along. It was some distance through the woods. The things I remember most about that walk in the woods were the crunch of the brown leaves underfoot and the sound of my little corduroy slacks. They were a lovely brown and made interesting sounds as I walked. Being at Mr. Riggens house wasn't so memorable. I think he had a cluttered home, as might be expected of a bachelor.

Another time we (Mom, Dad, Oneta, and I) were headed to

town in a Model T Ford with a single seat and took a different route than usual. I don't know whose car it was, but Dad was driving. We had to cross a small stream. The little car's motor got flooded and stalled. We had to get out of the car and walk to the nearest farmhouse, which happened to be the home of Archie Edwards. The lady of the house, Anna Edwards, came out to meet us. (I don't remember seeing her again for she died fairly young. Then again, that was a family we didn't have regular contact with.) Their daughter, Irene, who was a few years older than me, took my hand and led me to the house. Irene was Kenneth's cousin, and was someone I admired for the rest of her life. There may have been a boy a little younger than Irene.

Most of what I remember about that time is just individual segments, and not a lot of daily happenings.

It must have been about a year and a half after Donald was born that we moved to Salem for a while. Aunt Laura took care of Oneta and Donald, probably during the week while Mom and Dad worked and I went to school. Aunt Laura and her family lived several miles outside of town. My folks really had to push to get me into first grade, since I would not be six years old until January and school started in August or September. They promised to work with me so I could keep up. We did have to work on some things but I was able to keep up.

Aunt Laura babysat Oneta and Donald the year we lived in Salem. I thought for a long time that Donald was the one that had gotten in trouble there. He did get off to a kind of hard time getting into little troubles. But when I talked to Oneta in recent years she said that it was not Donald who had gotten into trouble there. It was her. She had urinated down the register that went to the basement furnace because no one would go with her to the scary outhouse. Oneta was spanked, spanked and spanked again. She was still crying when Mom and Dad went to pick them up for the weekend. The folks actually didn't like leaving Oneta and Donald with someone else. I know they appreciated the help, but as soon

PART I

as possible we moved back to the country and into a new house.

I remembered several of the kids from my first school year in Salem, when I ran into them years later. We had to line up outside before we went inside to our classes. The older kids had to line up too, but they were not in the same line that I was. There were Peggy and Billy Edwards, and kids in my class: Diana Dodds, Paula Dent, and Charles Whitmire. (These three were still in the same class as I when I returned to Salem as a junior in high school.) Mrs. Bingham was the teacher I had that year. She was a neat, rather large lady, but I don't remember much else about her.

I must have been about five years old when I got my first permanent wave. I had wanted to have curly hair, probably since I saw my first Shirley Temple movie. She looked so pretty and her curls bounced as she danced. For me, the hair-curling experience wasn't pleasant. The machine had a piece overhead with electrical wires hanging down and ending in a sort of clamp. I think the hair was put on a roller and clamped with the electrical thing. Well, I got a pain—maybe the spot was too hot. I reached up to rub it a little. Of course I burned my finger. I think the perm turned out fuzzy anyway. Maybe God didn't mean for us all to have curly hair.

We lived in different places with different people during that year. One family we lived with, in our own apartment, was the LeBrashes. Another family we lived with was the Weavers. Mrs. Weaver, Aunt Mary, was my Granddad Springman's sister. She had a number of children, as did my grandmother, but they were all grown by then. Several still lived at home. They were especially nice young women. I think that family had one boy and twelve girls.

Dad worked at the Rexall Drug Store at the ice cream counter. I got to stop in there a few times while we lived in Salem. They had ice cream parlor tables and chairs—the kind of wire back chairs with the nice rounded bends at the top. Of course the drugstore also sold regular drug store items.

Mom worked at Ely Walker, sewing either men's shirts or men's boxer shorts. She must have been really good at that for different times through the years when times were hard she would go back to work there for a while.

Note to clarify the chronology of early childhood family moves: We first lived on the 80-acre farm in the log house. We lived in town (Salem) for about one year while Dad was building a frame house that replaced the log house. At some point Dad traded farms with Granddad who had a 160-acre farm with a two-story house. These farms were next to each other. At some later point Dad bought an adjacent 100-acre farm (with the partial skeleton of an abandoned log house) that had belonged to his Grandma Russell.

Chapter 3

Hard times didn't bother us kids. In fact I think we did not know anything about hard times. Things were just what they were and we didn't know anything different.

I don't remember ever being bored until much later when we visited Grandma and Granddad Russell while they lived in Salem and some of us kids were there for the day. There really did not seem to be anything to do that day. I never figured out what we would have done at home but surely there would have been a book to read, a walk to take, or something to do.

I really don't remember much about the games we played as kids but there would have been spinning tops made by Dad from wooden thread spools, and hickory-limb whistles in the spring. There were a lot of farm things to do or try to help with. We always went barefoot when the weather got warm enough for us to not get sick going without our shoes. The green grass was soft and thick and there did not seem to be anything hurtful to step on when we moved back to the country.

The new house was bare bones. Dad never got around to finishing it. There were bare vertical boards on the outside, their lower ends uneven. The foundation was made of field rocks stacked under the corners and probably at places in between on the long sides of the house.

A Good While Back

At some point the edges under the house were filled in with more rocks, probably to keep small animals out, but sometimes a chicken would get under the house and not be able to find it's way out. Dad would have to crawl under the house to help it get out. The house was set in the same place and with the same orientation as the log house. It was just larger.

It had four rooms and was oriented with the short sides of the rectangle facing east and west. The south side was the front and faced the road.

The road, after several feet, turned north toward Granddad Russell's house. Across the road, on the east and the south sides, were woods. The trees on the east, probably what you would call scrub oak, were smaller than the trees on the south. Still it all felt cozy and safe. In the warm weather the wind in the trees was soft and whispered. In the late fall and winter the brown oak leaves rattled.

In regards to the house, the east end was the living room on the front with the kitchen behind it. My parent's bedroom was on the west end of the house; behind it was the bedroom for the kids.

I do not remember how we slept except that for the first few nights we had an adventure. We did not yet have a mattress for the bed for us kids, so my folks made a tick—which was a big bag about the size of a mattress—and stuffed it with straw or brown oak leaves. It was pretty noisy to sleep on so it did not last very many nights. We three kids tried various ways of sleeping that first night but someone's feet were always in the way. They must have found another bed. I only remember that one night of trying to sleep three in a bed.

After a while Dad put tongue and groove flooring in the front part of the house, but he never got around to putting the special floor in the back part of the house. Maybe that was because there was more furniture and stuff that would have made it hard to put new flooring in that part of the house. Besides that he had to make a living for the family. Tar paper covered the cracks on the walls inside the house. I do not remember if we finally had something different. We must have, though, because Dad put in a really nice colonnade between the living room and their bedroom. It was mostly open, with nice varnished framing all the way around. The "wall" on that side of the room had very little actual wall, maybe two feet along the ceiling and sides with about four feet along the floor except for the door opening. The door part was framed up from the floor for about four feet and had decorative knobs just larger than the framing to define it. It was very pretty.

We had a fairly large wood stove in the living room and in the winter when I got really cold I would stand by the stove, turning from front or back to get the other side of me warm. There was not much furniture in the living room.

Chapter 4

One year we had a Christmas tree in the living room. It was decorated and had clips with small cups in them to hold real candles. When the candles were lit the scent of fresh cedar mixed with the candle smell was so very special I will probably remember it always. We stood and watched the candles burn for only a very short time then they were carefully removed for we knew how very dangerous lit candles were on a Christmas tree.

One year the folks got a guitar for the three of us kids. I tried to learn to play it, but my fingers would get so sore from trying to hold the strings down it was just too hard for me. Of course there were no lessons, and I surely had bad technique. I sometimes wonder if they had noticed how much I wanted to try Aunt Laura's piano and this was a substitute.

At some time along the way they were able to get Aunt Molly Gibbs' (Dad's great aunt) pump organ. Wow! It had a really nice sound and I finally got to try to learn to play—without lessons.

The front bedroom had a nice bedroom set Mom and Dad had bought when we lived in Salem, and there was also a treadle sewing machine.

The kitchen had a cook stove, a washstand, and a table with chairs. Mom had plenty of pots and pans but probably the most used were the large iron skillet and bread pan.

I don't remember much about meals, except that breakfast was especially good. We had bacon with scrambled eggs, gravy and biscuits a lot.

Potato soup was another of my favorite meals. I later learned that this was considered poor people's food, but it is even still a favorite of mine. We all liked cornbread and milk, preferably cold milk. Milk was special and we always had a few milk cows.

We didn't have our own car. We used Granddad Russell's. There was rarely room for us kids to go along to town. One time when the folks were gone we were jumping on their bed (I don't remember ever doing it before or ever again) when there was a knock on the front door. It was a dark and rainy day and the man at the door wanted to borrow a shovel. He had gotten stuck somewhere on the muddy road. We were afraid of strangers and didn't know exactly where the shovel was anyway, so we didn't go find it for him. When the folks got home, Dad was displeased that we hadn't helped the man.

I remember one time when we did get to go to town. Oneta and I were allowed to go to Cobb's Variety Store. We were told not to touch anything. I don't remember if we actually put our hands behind our backs, but we were about that careful. I was especially taken with the delicate, embroidered ladies handkerchiefs. Mrs. Cobb came and stood across the counter from us, picked up the merchandise and let us touch it. She was very kind and I appreciated her efforts. The colorful handkerchiefs were and still are a favorite of mine.

Chapter 5

Discipline was a definite part of our growing up. Mom's weapon of choice (you might say) was a peach tree limb. They were small and limber and probably really stung. I don't remember ever testing it but someone must have, for things really quieted down when she told someone to get a peach tree limb.

I think Dad just used his hand for spanking. He really tried to keep on top of things with Donald. Maybe it was because one of Mom's brothers got into trouble and Dad wanted to be sure Donald knew better.

Even the animals just did not get by with certain things on the farm. One time Dad caught the family dog sneaking into the hen house and sucking eggs from the nests. I saw Dad take the dog into the woods. I heard a gunshot and I never saw the dog again.

I remember when Mom and Dad got new linoleum for their bedroom. It was a bright, pretty blue pattern. One time when they were out of the house I decided to do a little cleaning. I didn't like to be told to do stuff, but I had the urge to help when the house was pretty well empty. I probably swept the living room as well as the new bedroom floor and then decided to mop them. The mop we had was one of those where you pulled a lever, which opened a metal loop at the end where you put in a rag of some sort, then the lever would be raised to tighten the rag to keep it in place. When I tried to mop under the treadle of the sewing machine, the metal part holding the rag got caught on the edge of the linoleum. I panicked, pulled and tore out a tiny triangle of the new linoleum. Oh, my.

Guess what was noticed almost as soon as the folks got home—that tiny missing piece of linoleum. Naturally they thought Donald had been up to mischief again. Dad cornered and very roughly tried to get Donald to own up to the deed. Donald was really going to get a hard spanking.

I did some fast calculating, knowing I might get the spanking, but also knowing I might not, so I had to take the chance. Dad was squatted down in front of Donald and I touched Dad's shoulder. I said, "Dad." He said "What" in a cranky voice. I said, " Donald didn't do it, I did." Dad released Donald's shoulder and Donald got out of there really fast. Then I had to explain what had happened. He still wasn't happy about it, but I didn't get spanked.

We didn't have an outhouse, so we went behind the chicken house or into the woods and used whatever was at hand. Brown, dry oak tree leaves didn't make very good toilet paper. At night we had a chamber pot.

Even in what remained of the various former homes on our place and on Great Grandma Russell's place we could see an outline in logs several feet tall for the homes, but there were no remnants of any toilet.

Sometimes one of Grandma Russell's other relatives would visit. One who visited was a brother and his family. I think it was her brother Ed Hight who came with his wife and two kids. Like at our house, Grandma and Granddad Russell had no outhouse. When we girls needed to do our business we went a ways from the house and behind a brush pile. The girl cousin had a roll of bathroom paper. This soft, white stuff was something I had never seen before. It was a sort of a miracle. To me a Sears Catalog in an outhouse was a luxury.

Chapter 6

I met several of the older generation. I knew Grandma Russell's Aunt Effie and Aunt Molly. Even back then I knew they were interesting people. Aunt Molly was round and jolly while Aunt Effie was stiff and aloof.

We also knew Grandma's dad, who we called Grandpa Hight. Grandpa had no teeth by then so he would gum his food. He also wore no eyeglasses. He said he could see the stars so he could see as far as anyone. He came to visit at Grandma's house sometimes in the summer in those early years. We were there fairly often since we lived only a half-mile down the lane from them.

I also knew some of the older people from other sections of the family. I knew Uncle Will and Aunt Sarah Russell. Uncle Will was the brother of my Granddad James Valentine Russell.

I knew Aunt Mary and Uncle Will Weaver. Aunt Mary was a sister to my Granddad Frank Springman. I knew Uncle Henry and Aunt Laura Springman. Uncle Henry was a brother to Granddad Frank Rhinehart Springman, my Mom's dad.

I knew Aunt Hainie Coppedge, a half-sister to my Grandma Audrey Mae Springman, my mom's Mom.

Maybe all this sounds plain and boring but life was what it was and we didn't know anything different. There always seemed to be things to do or notice and possibly enjoy. I don't remember ever feeling deprived.

Part I

Several things about our front yard were special. There were a few flower bushes there. One was a fairly short bush that had small, pale pink blooms that were kind of doubled or with so many petals the blooms looked almost like tiny, fluffy roses. We had what I think was a Yucca plant with pointy leaves and pale cream colored blooms on a tall spike. Mom never liked that plant and tried several times to dig it up. We also had a rose bush that was really special. It was probably four or five feet tall with long draping branches covered in blooms of velvety dark red petals. It was beautiful.

There was also a very large oak tree off the corner of the house just past the rose bush and out a ways. That tree played into a couple of memories from that place. There was a clothesline that started from that tree. I don't know where the other end was attached, but never mind. I remember laundry being hung there in the winter and clothes being brought inside stiff, cold, and not completely dry. They were spread around on furniture to finish drying.

I also remember Mom standing by the clothesline reading a penny postcard she had received in the mail from her mother. Grandma was worried about several of the boys (her sons) having to go into the Army. She said she thought she would go crazy worrying about them. The year was 1942. Before World War II was over she had died and five of her sons were in the Army and one was in the Navy. They all came home safely except for Uncle Leo, who had a leg broken in two places from a machine gun that hit him as it swung around on a parachute as he came down in his own parachute over France. He was awarded a Purple Heart for the injury. There was a lot more to that story…and he always had trouble with that leg.

One of Mom's brothers who was in the Army (my Uncle Vernon) received a Silver Star Medal for bravery beyond the call of duty.

Mom's brothers did not talk much in my presence regarding their experiences during World War II.

Chapter 7

Our garden space was just inside where the road "cornered." It was fairly large. The soft, dark dirt seemed to make a really good garden. I remember seeing Mom busily planting something on the far side of the garden once in the cool early evening. At that time she didn't try to have the kids help in the garden very much.

It was such a soft, quiet time. It is a very pleasant memory.

The back yard was not well defined but there was a small peach tree up toward the chicken house and off the northwest corner of the house. Off from the cistern, near the house, was a gnarly old apple tree that had sweet, yellow apples. The apples from that tree were my favorites.

One of the ways we used the cistern was to cool our milk. We got white corn syrup in half-gallon glass jars with little bails—arched handles. (Dad always had to have something sweet at the end of a meal.) Sometimes we put milk in one of those empty jars and attached the jar to a rope, then very carefully lowered it into the cool water of the cistern. The cistern had a square wooden cover. I think we sometimes put a rock on it to hold it in place more securely.

One time while someone was drawing water a chicken spooked, tried to fly over the cistern, and fell into the water. Well, it had to come out or it would contaminate the water. Dad fixed up our swing, which had been cut from a car tire, with a rope to let me down to retrieve the chicken. I think I was tied into the swing so I wouldn't fall out. We must have had good rains; the cistern was unusually full. I panicked and could not go all the way down toward all that scary blue water to pick up the chicken. Oneta was probably the one who did it.

Another time the cistern was dry and needed to have the mud cleaned from the bottom. Again, Dad tried to lower me down to do the job. As before, I panicked and could not abide going down into that dark, suffocating place. Oneta and Donald ended up being the ones who could and did do the job. Oneta says Donald wasn't there, but I remember seeing both of them at the bottom of the cistern. Maybe Donald was playing around and they made him get out. Oneta said recently she wondered why I wasn't there to do the job. She did make sure there would be no snakes before she agreed to be lowered down.

Chapter 8

A chicken house on the incline above our house must have been the place for the medium size chickens. Off to the west beyond the oak tree and closer to the road was the brooder house.

In the spring we would order just-hatched baby chicks—maybe one or two hundred—through the mail. They were shipped in a fairly large kind of flat cardboard box that was divided into four compartments. Each of the compartments held twenty-five chicks. They couldn't be left at the mailbox, so to receive the chicks we either had to pick them up at the post office or meet the postman at the mailbox.

We had made a place ready for the chicks in a small house where they were kept warm, fed and watered. A sort of cone-shaped hanging hood was heated somehow to help keep the chicks warm. I don't remember what was used for heat and light. We didn't have electricity, but they had heat and light anyway. It was almost certainly a lantern.

The chicks' water source was called a fountain. It was a small round, metal tray that screwed onto a canning jar filled with water. When the whole piece was turned upside down, with the metal tray as the bottom, water gurgled out from the jar through holes and into the tray where the chicks could get a drink. As the water level in the outside tray went down, more water would come out of the jar and fill it.

Part I

The chicks were pretty with their bright yellow fluff. Sometimes we picked one up but they were so tiny and delicate we didn't really play with them.

It was interesting how the little balls of yellow fluff, tiny beak, black eyes, and skinny legs and feet went about getting their food. They had small galvanized feeders containing special ground grain within easy reach. But they didn't just get food from the feeders. They already knew how to feed themselves. They busily scratched and pecked among the wood shavings that covered the floor. They didn't bother with their little neighbors, so these busy little yellow fluff balls were going in all directions in their medium size space.

Beyond the house for the baby chicks was the pigpen. On the northwest corner of that was part of an old log building the pigs or hogs could use. That area was smelly, but I never especially noticed it unless I was really close. The hogs I remember were huge white animals that turned kind of pink in the summer, probably from the hot sun. They liked the mud puddle in their pen. Dad must have carried water for their wallow for they probably used it to cool off. That wallowing and getting muddy is probably why hogs got the reputation of being dirty animals. Our hogs were probably hogs to butcher. I don't remember knowing much about butchering until we moved to Granddad's place.

We most always kept what we called a slop bucket by the kitchen stove. I've been told that this was the cause of one of my first punishments as a very young child. Apparently I wanted to play in the bucket and got my hands slapped.

We didn't soak dishes and wash the dirty dishwater down the drain like we do now. We put used dishwater with the food scraps—which would have included things like stuck scrambled eggs and stuck gravy—in with the slop. The slop was mixed with what was called "shorts" to make pig food. Shorts was wheat that had been ground into something resembling coarse flour, but it was more brown because the bran was still on. Shorts was mixed with the used dishwater to make a slurry. More water or shorts was added as needed to make up the right amount. With the mixture Dad slopped (fed) the hogs. The trough into which the slop was poured for the pigs to eat from was made of two boards put together in a V shape with shorter boards to close both ends and provide stability.

At the west end of the pigpen was the remnant of some kind of log house. I wish I had asked what it had been used for. Dad probably knew what it was or even if it had been someone's home.

We only had chickens and hogs for meat except for wild game. Mostly that would be squirrels since we had plenty of them. When fried they were really good and very lean. Dad was always good at skinning the squirrels. He started at the back end under the tail, cut there and pulled the skin off like a garment. Then he cut off the head and feet to free the meat from the skin. He could do this without leaving any hair on the flesh.

Life really did revolve around the animals and the gardens and fruit trees. These growing things were what provided our food. It took work and constant attention to get them to the point of being ready to be harvested and used for food. Animals were fed or tended to twice a day, so that kept the farmer, Dad and sometimes Mom, tied pretty close to home.

Canning season was a really big deal. Any food that could be saved for the winter was canned—I think they call it jarred now. The food was actually cooked or pickled and put into glass jars and heat-sealed in a boiling water bath.

Oneta especially remembers us having to wash the jars. I'm sure I did my share but it was just one of the things we did to help.

Chapter 9

North of the pigpen was another apple tree. Its apples were not as good as the sweet yellow apples. I did climb that tree a time or two but most of the trees weren't really good for climbing.

A woven wire fence ran around our whole eighty acres. Another fence, made of split rails with the usual zigzag pattern, ran from a gate near the end of the pig house north over the rise to connect with another wire fence going east and west. I think the split-rail fence was going out of fashion by then but we had this one fairly short section.

Beyond the pig house and to the west was another oak tree. Under this tree Dad split off pieces from a round of a tree to make shingles for the new barn he was building. The shingles he made were thicker at one end than the other. I think the tool he used was an adz and it was fairly small. He placed it, then hit it with a mallet to chip off the next shingle. This had something to do with the water drainage system from the roof of the new barn. That was something else to remember and enjoy; I liked the smell of fresh-cut wood and that smell was created with almost any kind of woodwork.

There was a small pond nearby. Sometimes we would skim rocks on this pond and watch the ripples.

To the north of the pond was the hen house. It had a concrete floor, nests along one wall and roosts at the back of the building. We mostly had Leghorn hens back then for they were very good at laying eggs. There were boards with cleats (small boards attached at intervals for traction) for the hens to get to the roosts. The roosts were where the hens spent the night. They consisted of about six inch boards standing on edge and overlaid with poles six or so inches apart on which the chickens stood at night to sleep.

One side of the building held a section which was divided into open compartments with straw on the bottom where the hens sat while laying eggs. We always had plenty of eggs.

The hen house had to be cleaned out occasionally. Even with straw on the floor it would get pretty dirty. The roosts were especially stinky and dirty. When I got a little older it was my job to help clean the roosts. We used some kind of long handled wooden scraper and scraped the mess into a container to take it outside. The droppings were used as fertilizer in the garden or the truck patch. The truck patch was a separate garden with larger plants that needed less attention. It was farther from the house.

One year the folks wanted to get the hen house especially clean. There must have been mites or something on the hens. We scrubbed the concrete floor and fumigated the place by burning sulfur in the building. That is another memorable smell from the farm. The sulfur smell was kind of suffocating and distinctive.

At one time, north of the hen house there was an old rusting-out car. It had no top, no wheels, and the doors were sort of small and rounded at the bottom. We children played there sometimes. It was moved away at some point but I don't remember knowing what happened to it. The adults did things like that without consulting or informing me.

North of there were the remains of another log building. That building was about six or seven feet tall at least. At some time that building was also removed. I don't remember asking whose it was or what it was used for. Dad probably knew, for his Uncle George and family lived there before us. (I think Granddad Russell bought the farm from his brother when hard times caused them to leave and look for jobs in California. I think he saved it for Dad to buy later.)

Part I

Dad built a barn to the west of the hen house. It seemed different from Granddad Russell's barn; maybe that was because it was used differently. Sometimes in bad or extra cold weather we put the sheep inside the barn. If there were lambs that for some reason were not being claimed by their mothers we hand fed them. We used purchased nipples and we used what bottles we could find that would fit these special nipples. Of course we fed them cow's milk.

One year I claimed one of those rejected lambs as my own. That meant I had to go out and feed it first thing in the morning. One cold night the sheep had been put in the barn. The next morning when I went out to feed the lamb, I had to go into the room with all the other sheep. They had eaten wild onions the day before and that smell plus the warm sheep smell was very pungent, to put it mildly. Some of the smells from the farm were truly memorable but not all were pleasant.

There was a certain quality to the air on the farm that made it easy to breathe. Things felt fresh, calm and open. Things were calm and easy going even as there was nearly always something that needed to be done to make a living.

Chapter 10

Before World War II the folks decided to make a trip to Vinita, Oklahoma to see Mom's parents. We didn't see Grandma and Granddad Springman very often because they lived so far away. Mom and Dad decided to drive at night, probably so we kids wouldn't get too antsy. It was dark and rainy. We kids must have slept most of the way; it really wasn't an especially tiring trip for us.

Mom still had several brothers living at home, so the house must have been really full.

Granddad Springman worked at what he called the insane asylum. He worked in their dairy, providing milk for their facility.

Grandma and Granddad Springman's house was pretty plain, made of boards like our house. Grandma was a plain, busy little lady, looking after everything and everyone. There were other guests—some of the other cousins, I think. We kids were going to have to sleep on the floor. It sounded interesting so we started getting ready early. The adults didn't like us spreading old bedspreads on the floor, though. They took them up and did something else later.

While we were in Oklahoma we went to see the Grand River Dam. It was new and special in that area. We saw the lake and actually got to ride in a speedboat on the lake. There was a pretty good group of us and the boat seemed to me to be sitting pretty low in the water at the back. It almost seemed if we hung a hand out the back of the boat we could have touched the water. The whole trip turned out to be memorable and very enjoyable for all of us.

It seems like it wasn't much later that Grandma and Granddad Springman came to visit us. They took Donald with them as they visited other relatives in the area. He wasn't yet in school and he was a cute kid. They had given him a small leather coin purse and they got a kick out of (enjoyed) him showing it off and the relatives giving him a few coins.

A Good While Back

Chapter 11

We did have friends and neighbors. Our closest neighbors were the Salzwedel family. They lived up a little hill from us. Seems like the parents came from Germany and still talked with an accent. We kind of got off on the wrong foot with them, I suppose. Mom had a chipped enamel wash pan that she had taken out to the farm, probably when they were building the new house. She had left it next to the house intending to plant flowers in it later. It disappeared and she saw it later at the Salzwedel's house with flowers in it. I never really appreciated that family although they never really gave us much trouble, except I did get some teasing from the two children a little older than me.

In the summers, sometimes Aunt Laura and her family came to visit us on Sunday. The adults nearly always made ice cream when that family came. (We made ice cream with sugar, fresh eggs, cream, and milk. There was no worry about uncooked eggs or unpasteurized milk back then.) We had a hand-cranked ice cream maker with a metal canister that held a gallon of frozen ice cream. A long shaped churn and paddle piece swept the inside of the canister, which sat in a larger wooden bucket. The space between the canister and outside bucket was filled with alternating layers of chipped ice and salt. A contraption fit on top of the unit to turn the paddle and maybe the canister. A handle attached to the thing on top turned the can in the ice.

Part I

It was almost uncanny. When the ice cream was ready to be eaten one of the kids from up the hill would call down and say, "We're coming down to help you eat ice cream." Mom always took it in stride, got more dishes out, and we all ate ice cream together. (If she had invited them at an earlier time I never knew about it.)

For some time our only other neighbors were Grandma and Granddad Russell who lived about a half mile down a lane that ran along the east side our farm.

Grandma was not always kind to Mom. I guess she hated to give up her only living son. Even years later, at Mom and Dad's fiftieth anniversary open house, Grandma told Dad he didn't have to get married, he already had a home. Dad hadn't seemed like one to make a big deal of Grandma's little jibes; but when the time came that Grandma wasn't able to care for herself and Mom offered to take her in, Dad said no. Her youngest daughter, Lorene, took her in. Grandma got along better with Lorene than the others anyway.

On the other side of us was a house that probably was not as far away as our grandparents' home. A family named Kenney used it as a summer home. We saw them sometimes when they were there. They also had three kids. I remember them being at our house at dusk one evening, playing tag with us in the front yard.

Later the home of their cousins, the Harris family, burned, so the Harrises moved into the house where their Kenney relatives summered. The Harris family had several children younger than Oneta and I; the oldest was probably older than Donald. We walked home from school with them, but Oneta, Don and I continued on further. I remember one time Donald was getting pretty tired by the time we got that far and was crying. We had to walk a little more slowly the rest of the way home.

The Harris family had a radio. After they had lived there a while, they knew we didn't have one. On prize fighting nights when Joe Lewis boxed, they would turn up their radio so Dad could hear the fights. I guess the sound somehow traveled up the smallish hill and around the little bend, because Dad could hear the fights fairly well.

A Good While Back

Since no one had electricity in that area, the radio was hooked up to a car battery.

Part I

Chapter 12

When we moved to Granddad's place, there were neighbors on the other side. They were John and Johnnie Harrison. I remember picking blackberries with Mrs. Harrison one time. I think my Granddad Russell grew up with Mr. Harrison.

Sometimes when money was tight Mom would go back to work at Ely Walker, the shirt factory. She must have stayed in town during the week, for we didn't commute back then. Once, when Grandma had come up from their house—probably to check on us—someone must have suggested I make a cake. This would be a first. I think I was about eight or nine years old. I had been told how to do it, so I tried. My recipe was for a banana cake. It turned out pretty well…except that we had no bananas, so it was a banana cake without the bananas. I was teased about that for quite a while.

One time Dad decided to get a car for our family. He bought it in Salem. The car was an older model, and kind of boxy looking but it was a pretty, shiny black thing. We were just riding along back to the farm when a funny thing happened. I guess the car overheated. Dirty, rusty water sprayed from a hole in the radiator cap onto the windshield making it impossible to see the road ahead. Dad pulled the car to the side of the gravel road to check things out. We had to wait for the car to cool in order for him to drive it again because it couldn't be driven without water and perhaps the rest of the water would have sprayed out.

It was on this road that Dad was once stranded on one of his trips coming home when the tie rod ends came off, making it impossible to steer the car.

During World War II things were tight in places. Sugar was rationed, as well as car tires and gasoline. I think that it was that shiny car that Dad put up on blocks for the duration of the war; he used a wagon with horses or mules to go to town instead.

One year while we still lived at the other place, times were hard and he hired out at a dollar a day to stack hay for neighbors. He appreciated the money.

I'm not sure if Warfel School was there for Granddad and his siblings but Dad and his sisters went to school there. By the time Dad was ready for high school in 1925, Warfel had just started their two year high school. When Dad moved to Salem to finish high school, he took care of the animals for some people in order to have food and shelter. In this way he worked his way through his last two years of high school. He graduated from Salem High School in 1929.

School was special back then. From our new house on the farm we had to walk two-and-a-half miles to school. Part of the way we walked on dirt roads or cut through the woods to get to B Highway, the gravel county road.

In second grade I started Warfel School. That would have been the school year of 1938-1939. Our school was a two-room frame schoolhouse. The east side was the grade school and the west side was the high school. When I was in school we had one teacher for the grade school and one teacher for the high school.

Dad's youngest sister, Lorene, should have still been in school when I first started, but if she was, she must have dropped out for I don't remember her walking with me.

Oneta insists she was sent to school when she was four years old without getting credit for it. She would have turned five in November. She says that Lorene, Dad's youngest sister, was with us and wanted

Part I

to carry her. She also says the older Salzwedel girls, Stella and Lola, gave Lorene a hard time. She said we would wait until the Salzwedels were gone before we headed home, in order to miss them.

Back then girls did not wear slacks. To keep warm in winter we wore long underwear and brown cotton stockings as well as the usual outerwear. It was really hard to get the long underwear smooth at the ankles as we pulled up our brown stockings. I don't remember exactly how we held up the brown stockings.

There was one girl a little older than me, Naomia, who didn't have to wear the long underwear and brown stockings. She only wore anklets! Her younger brother turned out to be Kenneth, the man I married a few years later. Naomia and Kenneth only had to walk about three-quarters of a mile to school. Of course we later learned there was an explanation for the anklets. The cold didn't bother her like it did the rest of us. She even liked to go outside and break the ice on puddles in her bare feet. Her little legs did sometimes look bluish when she was wearing her anklets, though.

I remember walking to school alone on really bad, cold days when I was fairly small. I remember getting down in the ditch next to the road to try to get away from the cold on a bright and windy day. In recent years when we passed by that place I couldn't imagine getting away from any wind there, because by then the ditch was not deep at all.

Another time when the weather was really bitter, dark, and snowy, after I got to the gravel road—after taking the shortcut through the woods—a couple in a pickup truck with a stock rack on it stopped and insisted that I get in the back to ride the rest of the way to school. I saw that Bud Wofford, one of the high school students, was already there. After more urging and feeling a little more comfortable about the situation with Bud there, I got in. He didn't know the people either but we got to school safely and much faster.

Through the years I have heard some people say how safe it was where they lived as in St. Louis. In the country we knew to be careful of strangers. We knew the story of "little Marian Parker" who

A Good While Back

had been kidnapped, as well as the story of the Lindberg baby.

The classes at school were made up of children appropriately aged for different classes. They were held one at a time with the other students working on their own things and not minding the other activity. It is sort of surprising, but it worked.

We had a small library in the back of the room. The blackboard was on the same side of the room as the door; it covered most of that wall that also held the small library. The other side of the room held several large windows that took most of that wall.

The one and only door in our room faced the road and was toward the middle of the building. A partition in the middle of the building separated the grade school from the high school, and a small porch on the front covered both doors, one for each section. The grade school was on the east end of the building and the high school was on the west end. We, the grade school, had a table near the front door and to the right from the inside. I think we left our lunchboxes on that table and I think there was a water bucket with a dipper at first. Later there was a large crockery water fountain that had a spigot. We each had our own cups to get our own water.

Since Ken and I went to the same school at the time I asked him to help with remembering several of the details later.

Ken said we hung our coats on the middle wall between the grade school and the high school. This wall was later remodeled so it was a wall of doors that could be removed to open the space and use both rooms to accommodate large crowds for special events. I remember one really large pot-luck meal that was very successful. Many people from the community were there.

A very large wood stove sat in the middle of the grade school room. It was jacketed with a piece of medium-heavy metal that sat probably eight inches or so from the stove. The jacket would get pretty hot but it kept the students from falling against the hotter stove. The stove worked well to keep everyone warm.

Each student had a desk, which had space for books inside. The desktops had a hole in the upper right hand corner for an inkwell.

Part I

Because we used pencils and fountain pens we didn't need inkwells. The desks also had little indentions for pencils.

We had one teacher in the later grades who was especially proud of her two sons…and I'm not sure we ever measured up to their brilliance. The teachers were good and we rarely had a complaint. I don't remember there ever being any disruptions, either. Everyone was well behaved (in my memory).

We finally had a male teacher. His name was Max Stephens. I was really shocked one day when Barton, one of the Harris boys, was slow getting his drink of water and finding his seat for class. Max hit him on the head with a wooden ruler. It really bothered me. It was only later that we learned that Barton was mentally challenged.

Chapter 13

The Christmas programs in those times were special. We learned the usual Christmas songs and the Christmas story and presented something really nice for our parents and the community at Christmastime. We didn't go to church much then but in this way we were exposed to the Christian message.

At first we had tan curtains that we slid along a wire to close off the "stage" portion of the room. The stage was at what we used as the front of the room, or the extreme east end where the teacher's desk was. Later something on a metal roller was used to close off that section. The roller had a long metal cylinder in the center and was covered with a heavy material that was a little like oilcloth only it was heavier and had advertising on it. It was fitted with ropes to roll it up and down. It really didn't work much better than the curtain on a wire. Occasionally the ropes would slip out of place and not roll things quite as was intended.

The students exchanged names for gifts at Christmas. Once I got Bertha Brook's name. I knew what she needed. She had holes in the heels of her brown cotton stockings. So I had Mom get brown cotton stockings like I wore. She probably got her a couple of pair. Well, when Bertha opened that package and saw those stockings she looked at me with such disappointment in her eyes that I've never forgotten. Of course she wanted something pretty.

I'm still not good at choosing gifts.

Other events that were fun were the pie suppers. These were evening programs that must have been fundraisers. We always went.

Each of the ladies and girls made a special pie, decorated a box for it, and brought it to the school. Some of the boxes were pretty elaborate with crepe paper, bows and flowers so that made it very festive. The pies were auctioned, and the girl was supposed to eat her pie with the boy who bought it.

Oneta and I were not yet old enough to be interested in boys so it didn't really matter to us that Dad didn't want to stay very long. Because it was dark and we had a few miles to get home, he would buy our pies and we would take them home to eat. Sometimes we had coconut cream pies with meringue. They were really, really good.

Warfel School had two outhouses. The one for girls was off to the east and toward the back of the lot. It was a "two-holer" and we used pages torn from a catalog for toilet paper. It was a kind of scary place so I never stayed a second longer than I had to. I couldn't tell that they ever cleaned it out. The one on the other side—to the west—was for the boys.

There was a well house (which was a really small house that covered the well or cistern opening) at the east end of the school building. I do not remember if there was a pump; it was never my job to get the water.

Against the southeast corner of the schoolhouse was an Indian Peach tree. Oneta remembered that the peaches never became ripe. Students had to taste them to see if they were ripe before they ever became ready. I remember tasting one myself.

Some of the games we played at recess were tag, marbles, ball, and ring around the rosy. I'm sure other games were played, too. My main concern during recess was getting to the outhouse and back so I would be ready for the next study session.

There was a high school teacher who never got our names straight (Olieta and Oneta). She told of my trying to make Oneta keep her dress down. Surely it was during our younger years that

A Good While Back

I felt it was necessary to keep an eye on her. I must have been a child who was more interested in my own activities because I don't remember much about what my brother and sister were doing. It was such a busy time maybe it was just as well I wasn't trying to keep up with them.

PART I

CHAPTER 14

I had wanted a bicycle for a long time. I was never one to beg for things, so I tried to figure out how to make one myself. I did figure out how to begin building it. First cut wheels off the end of a log from a large tree…of course they would be really heavy. I never figured out the rest of it, or even how to cut the rounds.

One year Dad got a bike for the three of us to share. That wasn't hard; the bike had no fenders, which could be a problem for a girl in a dress. Besides, I lost a lot of my yearning for a bicycle after I really tried it. Oneta must have been of the same mind, because Donald used the bicycle the most. He had wanted it very badly.

Once when Donald had taken the bike to school he was enjoying it a little too much. It was a thrill to ride down the hills on the gravel highway on the way home. The first downhill was just as we were leaving school. There were sort of tracks where the cars had driven and most of the gravel was cleared away. I think that is where he started. But he must have gotten out of the track and into the gravel because he had a wreck. It was pretty scary and he was somewhat scratched up. The teacher drove him home with the bike and he wasn't hurt too badly.

A while after the trading of farms Dad bought a second farm that had once belonged to Great Grandma Russell. Once Oneta was riding the bicycle on the second farm. There was a lane between the one hundred and sixty acre farm and the one hundred acre farm. There was a barbed wire barrier closer to the house. Oneta didn't see the barbed wire and ran into it with the bicycle. She hurt herself pretty badly on that fence and had scars on her upper chest that showed even years later.

We took our lunches to school. In good weather we sometimes ate them outside. Oneta seems to think we had peanut butter on white bread sandwiches. That sounds about right. We felt sorry for Ethel Salzwedel, who was a little older than me. She had to eat bacon grease on homemade dark bread.

Some of the students in our school were Eugene, Louise, and Margaret Land; Louise and Cleo Larkin; Mary Lou Halbrook; Lloyd and David Land; Merl Asbridge; James Hofer; Henry Beasley; Kenneth and Naomia Edwards; Glen, Ethel, and Donald Salzwedel, Oneta, Donald, and Olieta (me) Russell; Junior and Muriel Land. Later there would be the Mortons, Betty Riggens, and the Sturdivants.

The Harris kids—Barton, Lavenia, and Jimmy—were with us for most of grade school but Mr. Harris lost an eye reroofing a barn and the family left. We later learned that Mrs. Harris went to nursing school and became a nurse to support the family.

We had to walk two and a half miles to school from the first farm and then three miles after we traded farms with Granddad. Most of the time we walked partway home from school with Louise and Margaret Land. Of course we talked and visited along the gravel road. Dad found a shortcut through the woods so sometimes we went that way to school. We had to cross a little dry creek that made so many turns we had to cross that thing three times. If it rained that was a problem. Oneta wondered whether we crossed on a log. I don't remember crossing on a log but I don't remember getting my feet wet, either.

One year the folks bought me a really special pair of high top shoes for the winter. They were plush lined and had a cute little fur-like turn-down top. They were very special; I may have even chosen them. One day after I had crossed the creek without getting my feet wet, a couple of older Salzwedel kids, Glen and Ethel, started taunting me, saying that my new shoes weren't waterproof. In my heart I knew they were right, but I let them taunt me into stepping into the water.

Of course my shoes were ruined. Mom and Dad got me a new pair, but they were plain, ugly, regular brown, high-top shoes. I didn't complain, but I had learned a really painful lesson: Don't let anyone cause you to do something you really know you should not do.

We had dirt roads that were almost impassable when it rained. The car's tires would mire down in the mud. So we never, ever got a ride to school in bad weather…or any kind of weather for that matter. Besides they really didn't want to spoil us.

Some of the teachers we had were Cleone Scouby, Bessie Bailey, Lenora Hunt, and Max Stephens. The high school teachers I had there were Reecy McGehee and Orla Vaughan. I always noticed the older kids who came to the high school when I was in grade school. Some I remember had also been in the grade school but were three or so years ahead of me. They were Henry Beasley, James Hoffer and of course Naomia Edwards. The ones whose names I remember that were in the high school but had not been in our grade school were Charles Wells, Charles Cox, and Ruthene Tipton. There were many others whose names I don't remember.

The first year I went to high school there were six in our freshman class: Louise Land, Elaine Warden, Bill Stephens, Leo Grogan, Merl Asbridge and me. My sophomore year, Bill went to Salem High School, and the incoming freshmen were Paul Brooks, Wanda Morton and Junior Land. We didn't have a sophomore class ahead of us. I think the reason was that Kenneth Edwards had been moved up half a grade because he had been the only child in his class. Then the family had moved to Salem for Kenny and Naomia to go to high school in town.

High school at Warfel was different from grade school. Of course the teachers treated us differently.

It was a lot quieter with so few of us. The room seemed brighter. The heating stove was a tall affair in the southwest corner of the room. It had a metal jacket like the one on the grade school side. Miss Reecy McGehee was our teacher when there was only the freshman class. Classes were not a lot different from grade school and, to me, not especially outstanding.

The sophomore class was different. Mrs. Orla Vaughan had a much stronger presence. Apparently she thought we got by with something with Miss McGehee. Mrs. Vaughan tried to set very high standards. She also read to us for several minutes several times a week and we were exposed to the poets and people who traveled, like Martin and Osa Johnson who were wild animal hunters in Africa, only their weapons were cameras. Henry Wadsworth Longfellow became one of my favorites of the poets.

Once the girls were standing by the wood stove and started bragging. First one and then another would say, "I told my dad…." When it was my turn I said, "I don't tell my dad. I ask." Somehow what I said got back to Dad and for some reason I did not understand then, he seemed pleased.

Once, Mrs. Vaughan assigned "The Barefoot Boy" for the group to learn. We were each assigned a verse. Smarty me decided to learn the whole poem. It was a long one and I had been assigned the last verse to memorize. I really had to work at it. When recitation time came it was very scary. I had barely finished learning the last verse. I got through the whole thing and I decided I would not *ever* try such a thing again. More than sixty-five years later I could still recite most of that poem.

One thing I find interesting is that those of us from our country high school (first two years) were just as well prepared as our city classmates for the last two years. When all was said and done I was third in a class of 65 or so at graduation at Salem High School.

Part I

Chapter 15

Mom was a very good seamstress. Several times during the years she made Oneta and I special new clothes for Easter. Sometimes there were hats and gloves. We surely must have gone to church to be dressed up, for the dresses were really pretty. She always made our dresses alike. One year we had skirts and tops made of a red print background with white stars. The problem was I had virtually no hips and it was difficult to keep the skirt in place. Another time the outfits, again skirts and tops were a pretty lime green with white lace. Once—not for Easter—she made a blue print into a circle. I'm not sure why this didn't work—it hung long on the sides—but maybe it was because of the hip thing again.

Back then some of the things purchased at the store came in fabric bags that could be used to make clothes or something else for the house. These fabric bags were flour sacks and animal feed sacks that held such things as shorts. We could pick out the fabric sacks with the colors and patterns we thought were the prettiest. We usually had some project in mind when choosing the fabric.

In so many of these events there was something to be learned.

Dad had to go see a neighbor about something. On the way home he had to cross a field owned by the Harrises. Mr. Harris had a bull in that field. Dad was wearing a really nice looking white shirt with a windowpane design Mom had made for him from a feed sack. We always heard about bulls running after something

53

red. Well, Dad found out they also chase after white. That bull chased him up a tree. I don't remember how long he had to wait for the bull to leave so he could come home but he was late that night.

Not too far away in our community was a country store and our nearest post office, named Doss. This was on Highway B. The store was owned and run by Frank and Iuta Alexander. The post office was in the back left corner of the country store, separated from the rest of the store and fixed with a little postal window. There the mail was sorted and then picked up by the rural mail carriers to be delivered on the rural routes in the area. Mailboxes were on posts along side the gravel county road.

We could get most things from the Alexander's store and didn't have to go to Salem (the nearest town and also the county seat). The store had all kinds of grocery items. On the left side as one entered by the front door, there was a pretty good selection of canned and dried products. There were also scales and the cash register, so this would also have been the side of the store where sugar and flour were sold.

The right side of the store held the dry goods such as shirts, overalls, shoes and things of that nature. There was a glass case about halfway back and on top of the regular counter but I don't remember what was in that case.

In front of the glass case were the bags of animal feed. It was here that we could choose from among the print bags.

In the winter their wood stove stood fairly close to the animal feed. I don't remember if they left the stove in place in the summer.

There was a small storage room back of the space where the stove and feed were. Out the back door there was a small porch and another, larger storage room.

Their outhouse was out in the back yard. It had a bucket of crushed lime to be put in the toilet as needed, and a catalog for another purpose.

The store also had a small gas pump. Mr. Alexander seemed short and walked with a limp. He would walk outside to the side of the

Part I

store, wind a little handle, the glass at the top of the gas pump would fill, and he would put as much gas into the car as had been ordered. The pump was taller than Mr. Alexander, cylindrical, and red.

Sometimes money was really scarce. One year while we still lived in the second house I was especially aware that things were tight. I told Mom and Dad I only wanted one thing for Christmas. I asked for what was called a comb case. It was fairly small, cardboard covered with faille fabric. It folded and had a snap for closure. Inside was a rectangular mirror on one side and a small pocket with a comb inside on the other side. They cost twenty-five cents each. They gave me a green one and Oneta a blue one. I do not remember what Donald received. One day I must have left my case on the bed. It slipped off during the night. Dad came to check on us and stepped on it, breaking the mirror. Again there was nothing I could do. Also, it would not do any good to complain.

Chapter 16

Someone, maybe a homemakers club, got together a community project. We gathered at the Melady's farm to make our own cotton mattresses. There were large, mattress size bags made of striped ticking—a heavy duty striped fabric—and cotton batting to stuff into the mattress bags. The adults sewed welts, which were small stuffed edging, around the top and bottom edges for stability of the soon-to-be mattresses. After the bag was stuffed with as much cotton as possible, the opening was sewn shut, then great deep stitches were made through the cotton mattress in rows up and down all the way across. Special buttons were placed at the entry and exit points of the stitches to keep them from pulling through the fabric.

They let me try to stitch, but it just wasn't something I could do. We children played and tried to stay out of the way. Oneta says they made three new mattresses for our house.

One year, John Hudspeth, who owned the field that the road crossed on the way to our house, decided he did not want us to go that way anymore because he wanted to plow that field and plant corn. He lived on B Highway so he just felled a tree across the road at that point without giving us any warning. It was a problem for a while, but before long we had a segment of a county highway that went along beside his property. It was a better road and we enjoyed the improvement. This road played into a scary incident we had a little later.

Somewhere along the way Dad bought our first mule team. Granddad Russell must not have had his team yet. Our team was a pair of old almost broken down mules. The male, named Toby was tall, raw boned, and almost black. His partner, named Jenny, was female, short, round and brown. They did well enough for the jobs that were needed.

One spring Dad built a cart for us kids. The cart was a wooden box with iron wheels, and wooden shafts extending from the box to what was the front for the mule. We didn't do a lot with it but Toby was our designated cart mule. He was really just too old and tired to do much, but cousins and neighbors came over to ride in our cart sometimes. It was a bit of a diversion. We had some of the Harris family ride with us, Louise and Margaret Land, cousins Junior and Muriel Land, Lorene, plus Oneta, Donald and I.

At this point in my story I think I may be getting some of the sequence of things a little mixed up but I am not sure how to correct it.

Along about this time Granddad Russell traded farms with Dad. Granddad had one hundred sixty acres and Dad had eighty. I don't remember that we grew very much in the way of crops on that farm. The ground had a lot of rocks. I think Granddad was getting old, or felt he was. Granddad and Grandma moved to town. I don't think they really lived on the eighty-acre farm much. Lorene would eventually get the eighty-acre farm. She had been around a lot to help and had married late.

One time we all had gone to Salem for the Fall Festival. At some point we were standing around, close to some benches. Granddad was sitting on a bench and the adults were talking. I looked over at Granddad. He was a kind of joker and at first when I saw him making a face I thought he was being funny. Not funny, he was having a stroke. He reached out his cane toward Dad to get his attention. Oneta said he tried to hook Dad's leg with the cane. Dad took one look and began to get help. Oneta said they got him to the doctor right away.

    I think that is when they moved back to the country for he was very sick and in a bed in the back part of the house when I saw him. His oldest daughter, Alma, was there and wanted to rub his head and forehead with her hand. That just made Granddad angry. Aunt Alma had some strange ways and she and Granddad didn't always get along. Granddad was in his middle sixties when he died.

    Granddad had been crippled (later said to be from polio) when he was a child and didn't have the full use of his right leg. He was of the same generation as President Franklin Roosevelt. He always rode a horse when he wanted to do much of anything. We had always lived nearby and Dad took care of Granddad's crops and jobs and then did for us. We used Granddad's team and Dad drove Granddad's car to town for things that were needed.

Part I

Chapter 17

One thing I was especially impressed with about the one hundred sixty acre farm was the deed. It was an original land grant deed.

The lane from the house on the eighty-acre farm to the other house ran along the straight fence line, made a turn around the barn then ran another, smaller straight stretch to the house on the other farm.

That road ended in a wide turn-around at the front of the house on the one-hundred-sixty-acre farm. A large tree grew sort of in the middle of the turn-around. The tree had an unusual sort of bowl shape in the lower part near the roots where Grandma used to empty her blue laundry rinse water (blue from the men's overalls). Any of their animals that came by had access to this water.

That house had four rooms and a concrete-floored, screened-in porch. There were two rooms downstairs and two smaller rooms upstairs. The westward downstairs room was the kitchen/dining room and sometimes Lorene's bedroom. The eastward downstairs room was the living room/bedroom. Granddad had built this house. He surely had help but there wasn't much that Granddad Russell couldn't do even with his barely-working right leg.

This farm had a cellar, a retired smokehouse, and an outhouse that Lorene added later, after she returned from a working trip to Streator, Illinois where she had stayed with relatives. It also had a well with a nonworking pump. There was a big old barn and a couple of chicken houses. There were gardens, one across the road from the house where there was a pond, and one behind the well.

The very best part of the farm was the wisteria vine at the front corner of the screened-in porch. The beautiful clumps of hanging purple flowers with their lovely smell helped make the porch special.

At the back of the house, opposite the screened-in porch and near the central partition were two doors, one for each of the two rooms. They were used mostly for ventilation, probably because there were no steps and it was at least three feet to the ground. I remember seeing Granddad lying on the floor, near the high door of the living room after dinner (what we called the noon meal). He would be resting and cooling himself after a hot morning's work in the field.

Another memory from that house was the time we spent the night there while Grandma and Granddad still lived there. We sat by the fire for a while and shelled corn from the cob for chicken feed the next day. It was cold upstairs but we had a feather bed to sleep on so it was cozy while Oneta and I were actually in bed. We didn't have ducks or geese, so we used chicken feathers. These separated but we were still cuddled in softness

I remember Granddad shaving in the kitchen near the middle door. He had a straight razor and used a razor strop as part of this procedure. He also had a small, chipped-edge mirror.

By the time we lived in the house we also used the doors for ventilation. One rainy day I was sitting there listening to the rain on a large cedar tree that was in the yard. It was such a pleasant sound and there was a pleasant smell of the wet cedar. It was then that I started trying to write poems. The first one was published in the *Salem News*, but they misspelled my name.

The poems were not always good but I enjoyed trying. To my mind there were a few that were outstanding and many years later we would self-publish all of them, mostly for our children.

Mom was really into canning. Oneta especially remembers

having to wash a lot of canning jars (again). I'm sure I did my share but I don't remember it being a burden.

One time when Mom and Dad were going to Salem without us, Oneta and I were assigned the job of getting a batch of green beans ready to can. Of course we had to wash the jars and get them ready.

We had to wash and break the beans and parboil them and get them into the jars. Our canner at the time was a large lard can and we had an iron cook stove that burned wood. This was a normal set-up for the time. I wrote a poem about that later.

A Good While Back

Bang

Bang, went the lard stand
Setting on the kitchen stove.
Bang, went the beans
And boy! They did explode.
Beans went to the ceiling,
Beans went to the floor,
Beans hit the windows,
And some went through the door.
Goodness, what confusion!
My sister sure was scared.
Of all the seven jars we fixed
Not even one was spared.
The floor was a chaos
Of beans, more beans and glass.
For a whole examination
Not a single bean would pass.
We swept the floor and ceiling
The very best we could
But if we should just look around,
Find glass we surely would.
Then the folks came home.
*(Boy! We were mad as heck.
For we were almost certain
We would catch it in the neck.)
After it was over
We discovered we were lucky,
For we had heard Lone Ranger.
Now wasn't that just ducky?

PART I

(Later I tried to refine it a bit.)

*Boy, we were scared you see
For we had no idea
What their mood would be.
After it was over
We discovered we had luck
We got to hear Lone Ranger
And didn't have to duck.
We were to break the beans and have
Them ready to be canned.
We thought we'd set them on to cook.
That wasn't even planned.
We knew the basic things to do,
But had never done before.
Perhaps we should have waited
And learned a little more.
Be sure there's water in the pot
And don't let it go dry,
For the things it can cause to happen
Could surely make you cry.
The walls in that old kitchen
Were pretty boards, you see
And that hot stuff sure messed them up,
Then brown as they could be.
I'd kept the old wood stove well stoked,
And burning really well
Then gone into the living room
Just to sit a spell
With sister and with brother
To hear our favorite show.
The story now seems funny
And it came out well you know.

The walls of the kitchen were narrow tongue and groove with the special beading. They were painted a pretty blue. The hot beans didn't help the look a bit. I don't remember if the kitchen ever got repainted.

When the folks came home Mom just got busy helping to clean up the mess, without saying a word. That was another couple of lessons learned.

After a while Dad bought another one-hundred acre farm. They had once belonged to Great Grandma Lenora Frances Gearhart Russell. Dad might have bought it from Uncle Will Russell, brother of James Valentine Russell, our Granddad. It didn't have the original homestead deed as did the one-hundred-sixty acres, but it probably had better soil.

My parents were simple in their needs and hopes. They had both grown up knowing about survival methods and ways to meet the needs at hand. There did not need to be any great striving to be someone great; they worked hard, played fair and were helpful to family, friends and neighbors. Truth was very important in their lives. They tried very hard to pass that on to us, their three children.

I thought for a long time that Dad must be a very important person in the community. I later learned he was respected all right, but was not really well known.

Dad was nice looking, always thin and could eat all he wanted. Mom was also nice looking and had a more boxy shape. She did not seem fat but she sometimes wished she were thinner. Her dad was that shape, and we do not have a choice in what we pass on to our children.

PART I

CHAPTER 18

One year after school was let out for the summer—surely it was May by then—Dad decided we should cut the sprouts from a field where he wanted to plow for a crop. This was on the one-hundred-acre farm. Apparently it had been used for crops before but little trees (the sprouts) had grown up here and there and needed to be removed. It turned out to be a cold day, but Mom was going to make it an adventure. She had taken a large Granite Ware coffee pot and although we kids didn't normally drink coffee we did that day. We had to grub out the roots of the sprouts as much as we could with a mattock. The mattock was a heavy duty digging implement like a hoe except more narrow and longer. It also had a chopping side flat like an axe but shorter and more narrow. It had a heavy duty handle about the same length as an axe handle. I probably didn't do any of the digging but there were other things to do. There were rocks to pick up and cut sprouts to move out of the way.

It started to snow after a while, a pretty, slow, gentle snow.

Mom found a quail's nest and she boiled those tiny eggs in that Granite Ware coffee pot, then we ate them with our picnic lunch. It helped make the day special, even with the family project of cutting sprouts to clear the field.

I do not remember all Dad grew on that farm but I think I remember corn growing near where we cleared and had our picnic.

That farm also had special features even though there was no house to live in. Up closer to the other farm house there was the skeleton of another of those log houses. This one had actually been Great Grandma's home. By the time Dad bought the place it only had the stacked logs of the outer wall still in place. There was a large plum tree near the house. When the plums were ripe they were sweet, pretty yellow, and a really good size.

Oneta and I both remember them. Donald is no longer with us to ask of his memories. He died at age fifty-five of lung and brain cancer many years after he moved to California.

There was a large pond close to the farmhouse that Granddad built. It had catfish of a nice size. We did some fishing from that pond. One year we had more rain than usual and the pond overflowed. That meant that a number of catfish washed out into what turned out to be a large puddle. We caught and used as many as we could but some died where they were.

We did have friends over sometimes. There was a larger girl in the neighborhood who came over a few times and brought her horse. She was handicapped in some way. I do not know if it was just a speech problem or something else but she seemed a little slow. I think she let us ride her horse with the saddle. The horse seemed really tall. I am not sure I rode it.

Another time I tried to have a party for the high school kids. I knew nothing about parties so it was a disaster. Another lesson.

PART I

CHAPTER 19

We learned to do many things while we lived on the farm. The cows still needed to be milked; I think we all knew how to do that. Dad liked to have help with the milking. I especially noticed it on cold winter mornings. I very much disliked getting out in the cold but Oneta didn't seem to mind so she was Dad's helper on those cold mornings…and maybe all the time. Oneta said recently that Dad really bragged on her. That was why she tried so hard to be his helper.

I didn't like the place where the cows were kept in the barn either. Dad didn't keep the barn really clean. He would shovel the heavy stuff out the window but it was still wet and dirty where the cows stood. (A while later we were to see a different kind of cow barn. We had some new neighbors move in at the place near the highway. City people. They built a new barn with a concrete floor. They cleaned the floor and put down fresh straw every day. Wow, what a difference!)

The cows in our barn had to be moved over somewhat so the milking stool and the bucket would be on solid ground. If a cow was a kicker we could use a hobble with metal clamps with a chain between them that slipped on the cow's back legs just above the knee joint. It was supposed to keep her from kicking and spilling the milk or getting her foot in the bucket.

The stool we used had just one leg…in the middle. I wondered about the balance of the thing and was told that the milker's two legs made the three-leg stance. I really thought Dad had invented that but later I heard of other people having them.

We milked the cows into a nice clean metal bucket. The buckets probably held about two-and-a-half gallons. When the milk was warm from the cow it wasn't as tasty. I liked my milk cold. The care of the milk was important. The milk was strained through a cloth to take out anything that might have accidently fallen in. When we brought the milk to the house we used what was called a cream separator to separate the milk and cream. It had a medium size metal bowl on top into which we poured the milk. As a handle was turned the bowl spun and the cream and milk then flowed out of separate spouts, separated by centrifugal force.

The cream was used to make butter. Some people had churns to make butter. We used a half-gallon canning jar with the lid on it and kind of sloshed the milk in the jar gently back and forth. We could see the butter as it started to form, and as more and more formed we sloshed the jar more gently to get it to gather in a larger clump. When it had pretty much all collected into one clump we took it out of the jar and put it into a bowl. The next step was washing it in cold water to get the rest of the milk out. Apparently the milk would spoil faster than the butter. Washing was done carefully by adding a little cold water and pressing and working the butter in the water.

Sometimes we would let the milk clabber (curdle) and made cottage cheese from it. The clabber was a sort of fermentation and had solids and a clear liquid. These were called curds and whey. The liquid whey was drained off and when the curds were heated carefully they would become more solid. This would be the cottage cheese. Then it was seasoned with salt and pepper and some buttermilk or maybe cream was added to it. It was really good. Fresh cottage cheese was one of my very favorites. I also liked the buttermilk if it was a little sour.

One time Mom learned how to make cheese similar to the American cheese we have today. The cheese was made by getting the milk down to the curd stage, then cooking it carefully until it sort of melted down to a soft, smooth product. Then color was added, and probably salt. It was then placed into something to mold it. It was very good. One problem was that we didn't have nonstick pans then. That stuff really stuck to the pan and it was my job to wash the pan.

Along about this time a new product came out: oleomargarine. The early version came in a bag and was white in color like lard. It had either a tablet or a small pouch of liquid color that had to be kneaded all through the white part to make it yellow. I don't remember why we bothered with it, but it was interesting and we worked it through and tried it.

Butter was better.

A Good While Back

Chapter 20

Sometimes the Stluka's (the people with the nice barn) would come to visit with their really old fashioned truck. They were pinochle buddies with our family. I assume they visited us to play cards but I also remember our walks through the woods in the dark when we visited them. Dad always led the way and carried the lantern. Since I was the one who scared easily I always got to be next. I am sure that Mom was always last, after Oneta and Donald.

One time the neighbors borrowed a hay rake from Dad and he volunteered us to go pick it up later. Don and I took a team of mules to get it. We had two teams of mules by that time—the old ones and a matched pair of young mules. The young ones were still pretty skittish so Dad sent us with one old mule and one young one. I was the designated driver since Donald was pretty small. On the way back the last small stretch of good road was downhill. The young mule spooked, probably from the rattle of the machine, and tried to run away. Don was on a brace bar next to the seat. I was so afraid he would fall off, the rake teeth would come down, and he would be badly hurt. We went really fast down that incline, Don held on, the hay rake teeth stayed up, and the team slowed before we had to cross that little dry creek. Donald was safe but my heart was really racing.

I don't know if it was before or after this incident, but one time Dad had been driving the young pair of mules. They were startled and ran away with the wagon in tow. It was at the last corner of the

Part I

lane just before coming to Granddad's old barn. The way ahead was a hollow that had a lot of young trees that had been cut off high— I don't know why, because that was not the normal way to cut down trees. The young mules headed into that mess. Dad decided to abandon the wagon and jumped off, taking his chances with whatever he found. He was pretty well bunged up, but he survived. He was more careful about driving those two as a pair after that.

Usually before planting a field or garden Dad would "break" the ground with a single blade turning plow. Here was another of the farm smells that I found so pleasant. The smell of soft, fresh-turned earth with the early spring plowing was unforgettable. After the earth was plowed the disk was used. The disk was an implement with a row of large sharpish metal discs that ran wider than a wagon. When this was run across the plowed field it helped break up the sod.

Then a harrow was used to break up and smooth the dirt even finer for planting. This tool had a metal frame with metal teeth in rows probably seven or eight feet across and about twelve inches deep. It was dragged across the plowed and disked field. Then after this, rows were made if that was what was needed for the crop being planted.

One year I remember seeing Dad plant a wheat field by the broadcast method. Maybe it was just a patch that year instead of a whole field, I'm not sure. As he walked along with a cloth bag of grain hung across his body, he would throw a large handful out with a sweep of his hand.

Since the girls were older, we had to pitch in and help with whatever needed doing around the farm. One year we got to help with the haying. I was going to get to drive the team and use the hay-rake. Donald could hardly stand it because being the boy in the family he thought he should automatically get that job. He was about eight or nine to my twelve or thirteen so there was really no contest.

That year we also got to drag shocks for Dad to stack. A shock was a small haystack, nearly head high to a child, which needed to be moved closer to the real haystack that was being assembled somewhere else in the field. The assembly was done by tossing the hay from the shock up to the person stacking the hay into a really tall and neat circular pile of hay.

Someone had to make the shocks first, but I don't really remember anything about that. Of course there was stubble on the field and at that time we always went barefoot in the summer. The barefoot thing was also a problem when dragging the shocks. The trick was to get the rope—which was attached to a trace chain that hung by a rope from the back of the mule's harness—attached on one side, tucked in, around, and under the edge of the shock with its dying plant ends, and back to the trace chain on the other side of the mule. The idea was to drag it, not turn it over.

Dad was always proud of his haystacks. They were always symmetrical, with the top perfectly round and centrically pointy.

We always went past the Carl Edwards place as we went to Doss or Salem. Kenneth's dad had a completely different theory on stacking hay. He liked to tilt the very top of the stack, thinking that would cause the rain to drain away better. Of course Dad seemed to think his way was best and always had a comment, thinking this was just inept, not knowing Carl just had different thinking on the matter.

One year a threshing machine came in to do it's job but I wasn't really involved in that. I think it would have been wheat that we had that year. It was dusty and loud so I just stayed out of the way. We didn't have very big crops and probably didn't need to have the thresher very often. We did serve dinner to the crew.

At least one or two years we grew cane to make sorghum molasses. The stalks looked much like corn stalks but they had different tops. Corn had tassels and grew ears. The cane had grain heads and the stalks had sweet juice inside.

Growing the stuff wasn't the problem. Harvesting was the problem. When the cane was ready to harvest, the leaves, which were like corn leaves, had to be taken off. That was called stripping cane (of course). This was the real problem because no matter how high your shirt collar was it was never high enough to keep off the itchy stuff that fell on you. It was a miserable job. Then the stalks had to be cut and laid in a bundle. I'm not sure but I think the grain heads were probably cut off at this stage. Then the cane was hauled off to a farmer who would continue the process.

Once I got to go along for the whole process. When all was accomplished it was a very tiring day.

There was a big wheel with an opening in the hub where the stalks were run through a press and the juice ran down into a very large, flat, rectangular type pan that was sitting over a large fire pit. The whole job started with someone putting a cane stalk into the slit for squeezing as the mule walked in a circle causing the wheel to turn and squeeze the stalk.

After the juice was in the pan it had to be stirred a lot as it cooked down until it was like syrup. Different times during the process the bubbles on top, scum (which looked green and ugly), had to be skimmed off and discarded. With the slow boiling and everything, the molasses turned out exceptionally well and light colored. Dad was really proud of the crop.

A Good While Back

Chapter 21

I first tried sewing when we lived in the house that Granddad Russell built. Of course I was going to use a feed sack or two for a dress. It had a pretty pink flower pattern. Mom had me use another dress as a pattern. I spread the dress on the fabric and cut around it. I did all right with it until I tried to finish the neckline. I must not have asked Mom how to do it for I never got it exactly right. I improvised and finally figured out something that barely worked. I did enjoy the dress and wasn't afraid to try that again.

I also tried really hard to learn to play the pump organ that the grandparents left when they moved. The organ was made of really dark wood. To me it was pretty and ornate. It had places with small woodturnings and little flat places that were small shelves that could hold a kerosene lamp. I don't remember ever trying to play the pump organ after dark, so I never had to try putting a lamp there.

Lorene showed me how to match up the shaped notes in a song book with the keys on the organ. I don't remember that she ever told me anything about timing or showed me how to read the many other notations for the music score. Therefore, I tried to play the songs I knew and worked with the tempo as I remembered it. Some days I would get started and work and work at the music. The family would often be in the house when I started but when I decided to stop there would be no one around.

They never complained but it must have been pretty bad.

Part I

We had a few outings that were different from the regular farm things. A couple of times we went on picnics by a small creek. I think it must have been south of Uncle Will Russell's farm. Once the Harris family was with us and another time there was a family named Plank who had a small baby. Those were really special times even if the water was almost too cold to do more than just wade. The creek was mostly very shallow and pebbly. It was an experience outdoors and we really enjoyed it.

One time we went hunting for pawpaws. They were supposed to be something like bananas. We went somewhere—probably a river bottom—that was damp with small trees growing there. We did find a few pawpaws. They were a green, stubby fruit, yellowish inside the peel with a few medium-size seeds. They tasted a little like green bananas. I think we went only one time.

Something else we hunted in the woods was a small berry that we called huckleberries. They grew in their season on small, low-growing bushes. They were small, blue and very sweet. They also made very tasty pies. We picked them different years.

Many years we picked blackberries. They grew in patches on long prickly stems. The berries were about an inch or so long and had little bubble like things called drupelets along the length. Each little bubble held juice and a seed, so they had many seeds. When we went to pick blackberries we tried to remember to wear a long sleeved shirt to keep from getting scratched. I think the long sleeves were also an effort to keep the chiggers off. We couldn't do much about the bluish fingers though, for the ripe berries were delicate and the little bubbles sometimes broke as we picked. The blackberries were used to make jelly and made very good pies if you didn't mind the seeds.

There had been a very large apple orchard to the north of the farmhouse at Granddad's place. It had been put in by Granddad Russell. Granddad had told us stories of the system he had used to store apples over the winter there. He would dig a hole in the ground in the orchard, line it with straw, fill the hole with many apples, cover them with straw, then cover them with dirt.

The orchard was getting old when we arrived but Oneta remembers there still being apples produced by those old trees. I don't remember it but she remembers Dad trying Granddad's old system when we lived there. It made a very strong impression on her.

There were also peach trees but they were in the chicken yard, which was to the west of the house. Those trees were small and scraggly. I don't remember ever picking peaches there.

There was a free-standing wall in that area that was about the size of one side of a small chicken house and one time Oneta tried to climb it. When it fell on her I had to get someone to help get it off her.

PART I

CHAPTER 22

Laundry day was somewhat of a big deal back in the early 1930s and 1940s. First we had to draw the water from the cistern or well with a bucket on the end of a rope. That in itself was not an easy job. When the bucket was lowered to the water it would just sit on top of the water. The rope had to be jerked to cause the bucket to tip so it could fill with water and be pulled out. Then the water had to be carried to the kitchen stove to be heated. At Grandma Russell's house, where we now lived, the laundry was done on the screened-in porch with the concrete floor. We used two round galvanized tubs that we set on heavy wooden boxes the size of small tables. The boxes were just the right size so the person doing the washing could mostly stand upright to start.

I think we probably didn't heat the rinse water. The white clothes and sheets were washed first in the tub of hot water using lye soap. We probably only did one rinse. We, mostly Mom, used a scrub board to help make sure the dirt all came out of the clothes. The scrub board was edged with wood and had small legs. It leaned against one side inside the tub. The middle part was made of metal ridges which themselves had ridges. The clothes were rubbed up and down on this surface to clean them. Sometimes bleach was used to help whiten clothes that needed whitening.

After the clothes were washed they had to be wrung to get as much water out as possible. The clothes were wrung by hand, twisting the item tighter and tighter to squeeze out the water. The next batch was the colored things. This was done without changing the water but just washing the lighter colored things first.

The last load was the overalls, dark shirts, and socks. On the farm men got really dirty and sweaty. Denim overalls were work clothes and they were heavy duty, kind of stiff and hard to scrub. They were also hard to wring.

I really didn't help much with the laundry. Mom had very strong arms and probably didn't trust me to do the job right, anyway. I probably helped more with hanging the clothes on the clothes line, but I helped enough to know the whole process.

For a few years we had the use of Granddad Springman's washing machine. Grandma Springman had died by then. Granddad was moving to California with his youngest son and wouldn't need Grandma's washing machine for a while. A gasoline motor powered the washing machine. The motor was started by stomping on a small pedal near the motor itself. It helped to not have to use a washboard, and the machine had a roller wringer. I certainly didn't get to use the wringer for I might get my arm caught in it. I probably didn't learn as much as I would have for Mom was very careful that we not get hurt.

A few years later Granddad returned to the area and needed the washing machine back. We didn't have one again until we moved to Salem a few years later.

The lye soap we used for the laundry was homemade. I don't remember the recipe but I remember generally how it was made. At first we used clean ashes (later we would use lye), pork grease and I'm not sure what else. It was cooked in a very large cast iron pot, out in the open. The pot was black and had a round bottom and tiny legs that set on rocks to keep it off the fire.

The mixture was cooked and stirred until it reached a certain consistency then was poured into a large flat pan and left to cool. Later it would be cut into "cakes" much like hand soap. When we had the use of the washing machine we tried cutting the soap into flakes to use in the washer but it didn't seem to work well, at least it didn't make much suds. We had to use commercial washing powder in the washing machine.

    Ironing was another thing I learned to do on the farm. We had what were called sad irons (flat irons). Ours were the sort of traditional oval shape. They were made of iron and they were heavy. We had two bases and one removable wooden handle. I had learned how to heat the irons on the cook stove in the kitchen but as in other situations, didn't have enough knowledge for the job I wanted to do. I had a nice rayon slip that was wrinkled from the washing. I wanted to iron it but I had the iron too hot and scorched the slip, making a brown oval shape on that pretty white fabric. Again, no need to complain, I did it myself.

    Some of my lessons really hurt.

Chapter 23

The cook stove naturally was a major thing in our farm kitchen. I'm sure we made fudge but the thing I really remember was helping pull the taffy. It was a kind of golden color and so hot you couldn't just hold it and pull it. You had to keep shifting it from hand to hand to keep from burning yourself. After we had pulled and pulled it over and over and it was cool enough and the right color and starting to feel brittle, we stretched it again into a fairly small round long piece. Then we would lay it back and forth on a greased pan to let it finish cooling. Later it would be broken into inch or inch-and-a-half pieces for us to eat.

Mom was very good at making divinity. I think she sometimes put walnuts in it. That is one thing I have never been able to master. She had such strong arms she could beat that stuff until it was just right. I can't do it even with a mixer.

The walnuts she used in cooking were also homegrown. You probably all know how walnuts work. We had to wait till they fell from the tree, then the green hull had to come off. It might be easier if they had dried somewhat and the hull had turned black, shrunken and brittle. Also this gave the walnuts time to dry and be a better consistency for baking and storing. After the hull came off, the walnut itself had a very hard shell. We used to find a good size rock with a small indentation, place the walnut there and hit it with a hammer. If you hit it right you might have some larger pieces of nutmeat. After cracking the shell we had to pick the nutmeats out of the little recesses in the shell. That sometimes caused the nutmeats to be crushed and made into smaller pieces. After all this the nutmeats had to be gone through or looked over to take out the little shards of walnut shells.

Mom made a very special applesauce cake and used the walnuts. I didn't end up with her recipe but sort of made up one for myself that makes pretty good applesauce cupcakes. Walnuts are good in those, too.

Mom also made very good homemade bread. It required a lot of kneading for it to raise properly and again those strong arms came into play. We didn't have it very often, though. We had more baking powder biscuits and cornbread. We had a lot of beans and potatoes and the cornbread was good with those.

Naturally we always had plenty of milk and eggs. We especially liked cornbread and milk as part of our supper.

Many times early spring brought a treat. Mom knew which of the early wild greens were edible. I still remember a few: poke, dandelion, narrow dock, and I think wild lettuce. When these were cleaned, cooked and seasoned with a little vinegar they were especially good.

A few times we also found wild strawberries. These berries were pretty, tiny, bright red and very sour. They had leaves similar to their store-bought cousins and I was able to recognize them years later in another place.

Chapter 24

After World War II was over Mom's brothers all came home. Mom had six brothers in the service at that time. Billy was an aircraft mechanic, in the Army; Delbert was in the Navy; Ed was in the Army in the Aleutian Islands (off the coast of Alaska); Leo was an Army Paratrooper who was injured over France; Vernon was in the Army; Carl Ray was drafted toward the end of the war and did not actually see active duty.

Uncle Vernon stopped by to visit us before he headed to Nevada (I think it was). His pretty wife, Lois, and his very small son were with him. My little cousin couldn't have been more than one-and-a-half or two years old. We were going to have fried chicken for the noon meal. Again Mom would put her strength to work. To kill the chicken she wrung it by it's neck by swinging it in a big circle. It always worked for her.

We had some little yellow chicks in the fenced back yard just walking around doing their thing. I looked out and guess what. There was little Randy with his little hand around the neck of one of the chicks and starting to swing it just like he had seen Mom do. Some of the adults rushed out to save the chick. The chick was not seriously hurt but was somewhat stunned and staggered around for a while.

Uncle Vernon was one of the heroes of World War II. The way I remember the story, he got tired of their group being tied down by gunfire and stormed a German gun emplacement single-handedly and helped save his group of soldiers. He was awarded a Silver Star for his bravery.

I think Uncle Vernon gave his peaked cap to Donald.

Uncle Delbert came by once or twice and gave Donald one of his sailor hats. My uncles seemed to visit Aunt Laura more. I'm not sure why, because her road was much worse than ours, it seemed to us. Her road was like a washboard with a lot of ridges. Our road was hard to travel when it was rainy but it wasn't rainy all the time. Maybe it was because Mom was more quiet and sensitive and wasn't as talkative as either of her sisters. She was never a big talker but she could do anything she set her mind to do.

We never lived close to the Springman side of the family, so it was always special when we saw any of them. Most of the uncles and aunts came by sometime or another.

We always lived close to the Russell side of the family. I guess Dad felt a special need to be a help to his dad. There were originally seven children in that family but only four lived to be adults. They all lived fairly close except Lorene who lived a year or so in Streator, Illinois with her mother's Aunt Effie Harris. It was a good experience for her. Lorene married a little later than the others in her family and it was a bad marriage overall. One of the things her new husband told Dad was "what's yours is mine." He meant it.

Another of the relatives we got to know was Aunt Molly Gibbs. She was sister to Aunt Effie and Great Granddad George Hight.

I enjoyed knowing some of these older relatives.

One of Dad's stories was of being small and receiving hand-me-down clothes from a son of Aunt Molly. Grandma made him wear short pants to use up these clothes while other boys Dad's age were getting to wear long pants. That apparently was really hard on Dad.

Chapter 25

We were home from school one time when they butchered a hog. I don't remember who came to help but it was a major production. They had a big pot of boiling water for scalding the hog so the hair could all be scraped off. I heard the gunshot. That indicated the animal had been killed. In retrospect, I guess I don't remember the exact sequence of their system. Which was probably a good thing. The hog had to be bled first and there was gutting, scalding, scraping off the hair. At some point the hog was raised by a pulley and hung by its rear feet.

After that the hog had to be cut up into sides of bacon, hams and shoulders. These were salted down and stored. Sausage was made but I don't remember how it was stored. Some of the meat was canned in regular canning jars. The head was boiled and the meat and brains taken off/out. I especially liked cooked pork brains. The sliced salt pork and ham were very good too.

I don't remember that we ever used the smoke house beside and over the cellar on Granddad's place. I think that by the time we moved there that space was being used for storage. I do remember seeing old clothes in boxes there.

One year we tried to raise big, fluffy, tame rabbits. It must not have been very successful for that project didn't last very long. They may have needed more delicate care than the other animals we were used to raising. I don't remember if we finally killed and ate them.

Part I

In those times, growing and harvesting your own food was very important, as it would be later, in the early years of my own marriage. It was a matter of survival and was just a part of daily life. That was another major lesson of life. Work was just something you did.

Chapter 26

When I graduated from Warfel High School after my sophomore year we had to figure out what came next for me. Louise Land and I wanted to stay in Salem with her Aunt Juanita Vaughan. She had a spare room and her house was within walking distance of the high school there. Juanie was a really nice lady and apparently didn't mind having us. Her husband, Seymore, was still alive at the time so she wasn't alone and she probably really didn't need the company, but that was okay.

We stayed in town during the week and went home on weekends. We must have taken care of our own meals for I don't remember that we ate with the Vaughans. It really wasn't a very exciting time.

Louise made friends easily at school. She soon became friends with the cheerleaders and the prettier girls. I just didn't seem to fit in. In my junior year the principal, Helene Bircher, asked me to work after school helping with the attendance records. It only took about an hour a day and I received $2.50 at the end of the week.

Some of the teachers my dad had when he went to Salem High School were still there and I had those same teachers. Two I especially remember were Miss Bircher and Miss Alice Dent. They were still very good teachers and I remember them fondly.

Miss Dent taught history. My first test in that class was interesting. It was a True/False test. The questions had little blanks before the question for the T/F answer. I didn't know all the answers, so I

PART I

went through them and answered the ones I knew. Then I noticed a pattern. I went back over the test and filled in the ones that were still empty according to the pattern I had noticed. I got 100% on that test. I never detected patterns in our tests again that year. I looked for them.

The classes were interesting and I did enjoy the learning. I'd had Algebra I at Warfel but didn't have Algebra 2 until my senior year, and by then I had lost all the basic understanding I had from the earlier class. I got a good grade, but I didn't fully understand the concept anymore.

With a few exceptions, Louise and I got along together very well. She didn't like the way I wanted to arrange a special dresser set that had a mirror, hairbrush and comb. I wanted the brush with the bristles up so they wouldn't get bent. She wanted the bristles down so the pretty back showed. She kept changing it from the way I had it.

We had to carry water from Jaunie's kitchen to wash our dishes. One day after I filled the dishpan with water I pretended to keep Louise from using it by holding the handle for the faucet. She decided she was going to use it anyway and grabbed my hand and tried to get what she wanted. It hurt my hand quite a bit and I was ready to give in but somehow I didn't say the right words. I was wearing a special new ring that I had bought for myself. It was thin gold and fragile so naturally it got crushed and mangled.

I was very upset about my ring and when I went home that weekend I cried and worried all weekend. When it was nearing time to go back on Monday I decided I had to bite the bullet and go on back to stay with Louise. However, my folks had other plans. Somehow they had found another place to stay and Mom stayed in town with me the rest of that year. How was that for independence...staying with my Mom?

By the time my senior year rolled around Mom and Dad had a new house almost built and we all moved to Salem.

Oneta remembers that she and Donald helped Dad cut the logs

to take to the mill to make lumber for the new house. I think the way they did that was to take the logs to the mill and exchange them for cured boards to build with. They must have done that the summer between my junior and senior years of high school. I worked at Parker's News Stand that summer so that would be why I wasn't involved with the preparations for the new house.

I hated it that they had to sell the farm in order to move to town. Dad was surprised when I told him. I don't know if I had complained about the farm or why he thought I wouldn't mind.

He had the original homestead deed for the farm and for some reason that was important to me. They always seemed to do things without letting us know what they were planning. It probably wouldn't have made any difference in their decision making, for they did things they thought were best. Maybe this was best for them. By this time Dad was working with a carpenter and the money was better. Maybe not having to deal with trying to earn a living on the farm was better for them.

When they retired many years later they bought another farm in Dent County. Although Ken inherited eighty acres later from his parents, it never seemed logical for us to move back to the farm.

I finished High School in May of 1949. I didn't make Valedictorian or Salutatorian but came in third in class standing. I was supposed to write a speech and be one of the speakers for the commencement exercises. I didn't really know how to write a speech so Miss Bircher wrote the speech for me. I guess it turned out all right. It was just one of the many "firsts" in my life where I had never seen or heard about something and the first thing I knew of it was my own experience, so I had to learn from there.

I worked at the Parker's News Stand the summer before my senior year in high school and part of the next summer, also. The second summer was sort of anticlimactic and wasn't as exciting as the first summer. That first year I saved enough from my earnings to buy Oneta and me new winter coats for my senior year and her sophomore year in high school. I did not make enough to have money for a coat for Donald but there was nothing I could do about that. We chose our new coats from the Montgomery Ward catalog. With the three dollars I had left, I bought a small (really small) medicine cabinet for the bathroom in the new house.

When we got settled in the new house Oneta and I started to church and Sunday school. We went to the First Baptist Church in Salem. I think it was during the fall revival that I felt a little call and decided to accept Christ as my Savior. There was so much noise with the loud singing that it was all very confusing and no one gave me any kind of special instructions. A little while later I was baptized and joined the church.

Many years earlier, we had attended a revival led by Rev. Virgil Parker at Antioch school or church near Max, Missouri. (I thought it was a school but recently Louise said there was also a church there.) During that service I had felt a warmth and a deep peace and knew I belonged to Jesus. That feeling hadn't left me, but during the service at Salem it seemed to be the time to make a public confession.

Chapter 27

After I was baptized Kenneth Edwards asked if he could drive me home. Mom and Dad had already agreed to meet Oneta and me to drive us home, so I had to tell him no.

Soon after that he asked me for a date.

I started dating Kenneth during my senior year in high school. I think it was in November that he had his sister buy a pretty string of really nice fake pearls for me at Famous-Bar in downtown St. Louis. She was working downtown at a bank. I think the bank was Boatman's.

Kenneth and I became engaged in February of my senior year of high school. There were two couples who married during my senior year but I think they must have been older.

After graduation I got a job working at what was named the Ely Walker Shirt Factory. Actually, they made shirts and boxer shorts. They put me to work on a double needle sewing machine doing the curved seam in the back of men's boxer shorts. That kind of seam was where the fabric was turned under at the bottom and also turned under at the top to make a very nice, precise seam. It was supposed to lay nice and smooth.

Somehow or other it just didn't work for me. I kept catching extra fabric when I tried to make the curve, and when the seam was not right it had to be taken out and done again to get it right.

A little while after Ken and I were married I lost my job.

Part I

Some comments were made during my early writing of this memoir indicating I should include more personal comments and stories about my understanding of the times and ways then. The truth is, I was probably just carried along with what was happening and what needed to be done and really did not do any deep thinking. As far as I was concerned, things were just the way they were supposed to be. I did not have anything to compare to what was later called "hard times," so there was nothing to fuss about or worry about. We just coped, made do, did without, and improvised where needed.

We always had enough.

I did notice that Aunt Laura and her family had a nicer house, but Mom never made a fuss, probably because she had married the man she loved and the circumstances that came with that were just a part of life.

When life and events improved later we just took it in stride, too, and enjoyed our good fortune or blessings.

A Good While Back

Ray and Myrtle Russell

Ray, Myrtle
Olieta, Donald, Oneta Russell

From Left: Olieta, Oneta,
Donald Russell

Part II

A Good While Back

Part II

Chapter 1

Kenneth Edwards and I were married on November 11, 1949, in Salem, Missouri. That day was a holiday, called Armistice Day at that time, now Veteran's Day. It was a very nice day for so late in the season. We chose that day because Ken's sister, Naomia, lived and worked in St. Louis and would have to come home by bus. She said she wouldn't believe we were married unless she was there to see it. I was seventeen years old but would turn eighteen in January. Ken was nineteen the September before the wedding.

We had been engaged since February and it seemed like it was time to be married. Since we were both under age we had to take both of our mothers with us to sign the papers so we could get our marriage license.

I was very unsophisticated, just fresh from the country, and really didn't know very much about anything. I had never been to a wedding. Although we had been invited to the wedding of my cousin, Melba Haas and her fiancée, Joe Parker, we hadn't gone. We probably didn't have nice enough clothes to wear and maybe couldn't afford a nice wedding gift.

I had seen a picture of Mom and Dad from about the time of their wedding. Mom was wearing a really pretty dress, but it wasn't white. I guess I thought it was her wedding dress. I did not think to ask. There have been many, many times in my life when I did not ask enough questions.

A Good While Back

We had a simple wedding in the church parlor of the First Baptist Church in Salem. It was in the early evening with our brothers and sisters there as witnesses. Oneta was my bridesmaid. Ken's cousin, Jim Edwards, stood up with him as best man. Rev. L.M. White performed the ceremony and Mrs. White was there as well as their daughter, Marigene.

My dress was slate blue slipper satin. It had a plain overhang for sleeves and a really pretty drape effect over the mid section ending in a sort of flattened bow in the back. The dress had a zipper in the back and came to about mid calf. Ken's suit was blue. He wore a white shirt and striped tie with it.

Mom and Dad didn't go to the wedding but stayed at home where we would have a small reception with refreshments. Ken's folks didn't go either but went on over to my folk's house and waited there for us to finish at the church. First though, we stopped by Mrs. Alexander's photography studio to have wedding pictures made. These pictures were black and white; we didn't have her do any sepia work, tinting, or photo oils. Years later we did some copy work and used photo oils and sepia tones for a more updated look.

We all met at Mom's and Dad's after the pictures. Mom had made a two-layer angel food cake. She had made the larger layer in a new aluminum dishpan she had bought especially for this purpose. The cake had white icing and little bride and groom figures on top. We had punch and sat around and visited. (We got the dishpan for our new apartment.)

As a special surprise, Ken and his Mom had fixed the upstairs at their house into a pretty little apartment. The space was up under the slanted part of the roof and felt rather confining but there was a nice cabinet. I am not sure about a sink, and there must have been a table and chairs. The bedroom was also under the eaves but had a nice wooden bedroom set. The rooms were separate as they would be later in some of our other apartments.

This setup really didn't feel comfortable to me. I didn't know how to cook or plan meals for my new husband so it wasn't long before we were eating downstairs with his parents.

As you can guess this wasn't really a desirable situation.

One night soon after we were married there was a loud banging of pots, pans, and buckets after we had gone to bed. I had no idea what was going on. I put on my robe and started downstairs. Ken's Mom was there and had me go back upstairs and get dressed.

It was a chivaree. I had heard of them but had never been involved in one. I think they were not as common at this time as they had been previously. After all the racket Ken's Mom invited everyone inside and served cake and coffee.

Mom had been doing home permanents for me and probably for Oneta. I think I had been doing Mom's hair, too. I did try to be helpful, and one of the things Ken's mother, Daphnia, asked me to do was give her a home permanent. I don't remember if I did more than the first one, but at least that one turned out fuzzy. When it needed to be rinsed out to fix it for permanency she insisted we have lunch first. The result was that it was overdone and fuzzy. But she never complained.

I was scant on sexual training and when things didn't progress as Ken thought they should he said he was moving back to his old bedroom. I had lost my job at Ely Walker by then so I was home that day. I wasn't ready to give up on things so soon, so while the others were at work I took the bed apart in our new bedroom and stored it in the little space under the eves next to the bedroom. That night I still slept with my new husband…but in his old bedroom in his old iron frame bed.

Jobs did not seem plentiful in Salem at that time. Ken lost his job as a box maker at Ely Walker soon after I lost my job. For a little while we sort of sat around the house, not quite knowing what to do about our situation or how to improve it.

Chapter 2

Early in the spring of 1950, Naomia suggested we move to St. Louis where she lived in a rooming house with their Aunt Lennie Smith. There was a room available in that house so one weekend we took the bus to St. Louis. Naomia and Aunt Lennie met us at the bus station.

The room really wasn't much but we were finally on our own. This was 1730 Nicholson Place, off Lafayette Street as it went past Lafayette Park. The room was on the second floor and had a bed, a dresser, a table with two chairs, a very old cook stove and a dish cabinet. It was sort of on the corner of the building and had two windows, one on the front of the house and the other sort of on the side. The refrigerator was in the hallway and we shared it with the people on the third floor. The bathroom was down the hall and the laundry facilities were in the ancient basement. This place cost us five dollars a week.

We planned to look around St. Louis before we seriously started our job searches. We had arrived on a Sunday and on Monday morning, Ken's brother, Wilber, slipped away from work at Brown Shoe Company to take Ken in for an interview. Ken started to work for Brown Shoe Company the next day. It was a Union job that would turn out advantageous even years later.

My Uncle Bill Clinton, who was married to Mom's sister, Hildred, took me in his car to American Associated Insurance

Part II

Companies for an interview and I started to work there. During the interview I was asked if I was planning to get pregnant soon. I told the lady I wasn't planning on it. What struck me as funny later was the fact that she was the one to get pregnant first. I went to work soon after Ken started his job and I ended up working there about a year and a half.

Ken and I were still pretty ill at ease around each other. I especially was trying to please him. We were just learning to shop for food. I was trying to learn what he liked to eat and how to cook. Also we had to take the bus "home" every weekend. This continued for a very long time. Ken was very close to his mother and maybe he felt he was abandoning his first best girl. It was many years before I really began to feel comfortable in this relationship. It wasn't just his mother but it was a long time before I felt he seemed to actually see me as a helpmate and partner.

We settled into our new jobs and seemed to do okay. We both had to take the bus to work. My job was on Fourth and Pine, near the Mississippi River in the Pierce Building. It was catty corner to the Old Cathedral at the back and we could sometimes hear the calliope on the Showboat on the Mississippi River.

The ladies I worked with were nice, but it took me a while to learn to be friendly and comfortable with people. One young woman, was probably about my age and worked nearby. I later learned she had wished I was friendlier. I guess I was slow learning a lot of things.

When it was time to do laundry I had to go to the basement to light the water heater first. Back then it seemed important to have hot water for the laundry. One of our neighbors on the third floor figured out when there would be hot water and would rush down to the bathroom and take his bath then. I finally realized what he was doing and one day just didn't go downstairs to start the laundry at the usual time. Again, he rushed down for his bath. After he finished I went to the basement to start my laundry. He never tried to take my hot water again.

A Good While Back

While we lived on Nicholson Place one of our neighbors got a television. These people were friends with Naomia and were a little older than us. After a few days we got to see it but we didn't want to impose so we didn't sit down to watch a program. Here was this picture on this little screen, probably seven inches. Still, it was rather impressive. It was many years later before we had our own television, and it was much larger.

Time moved on as we tried to get used to some semblance of married life. Kenneth liked his early morning newspaper. It was *The St. Louis Globe Democrat* at the time. He sat in his rocking chair smoking his pipe, and reading his newspaper every morning before work. It almost seemed like this was to make himself seem older.

To me it was so much better being on our own even having to go "home" every weekend. I gradually learned to cook a few things. I had had Home Economics in high school and knew a few things about diet and food prep. I surely picked up some things from Mom regarding cooking, too. I also learned some things about sewing as I was growing up and in Home Economics. I didn't get into sewing at that point but that knowledge would come to be helpful later.

Since we were both Southern Baptists we both assumed that Kenneth would lead out in our marriage. It was a little later when I especially noticed that he took the role seriously. While most of the time he did not seem to be "boss" there were times when he would make a decision without consulting me. While I never challenged him in public there were a few times that I gave my opinion later. While the decision was rarely changed, gradually through the years it allowed for a chance to voice my opinion earlier.

Ken made our first bookcase while we lived on Nicholson Place. He had taken apart a crate at work, brought home the boards and made the bookcase. He didn't have many, or possibly any, tools to work with. He may even have borrowed them. The case was rough but was very useful and we still have it after at least sixty-two years. We finally did paint it but it was never sanded and smoothed.

We got our first car while we lived on Nicholson Place. It was

PART II

a nice looking black 1939 Ford. Since Ken was underage, his dad had to sign to get the car. It meant we no longer had to take the bus when we went "home" for the weekend.

We arrived in St. Louis just as they were phasing out streetcars. We may have traveled a few times that way, though. Ken thought some of his first times to go to work involved taking a streetcar.

We lived on Nicholson Place for about a year and a half, until I became pregnant with our first child. Ken had good medical insurance by then through the Teamsters Union. We moved to our second place in St. Louis in November 1951. It was two rooms on the second floor of 1619 Pennsylvania Avenue. Again it was less than ideal. The two rooms opened to the hall and were not connected to each other. The bathroom was in the hall and the laundry facilities were again in the basement.

Chapter 3

I quit my job at American Associated in November, after working there a year and a half. I expected that to be three months before the delivery of our first baby. I don't know why I quit early but it turned out fine anyway. I didn't have to go to work on the bus during a big snowstorm soon after I quit.

I hadn't gained a lot of weight. Actually I started out weighing about 103 pounds and two weeks before the baby was born I weighted 111 pounds. Dr. Forrester seemed pleased with the low gain.

I don't remember exactly when my contractions started but it was well up into the day when it seemed like it might be a good idea to go to the hospital to get things checked. The pains weren't severe, so when Ken pretended to speed to St. Mary's Hospital, I told him he probably didn't need to rush, that it was probably nothing. He still wanted to hurry, just in case he didn't get another chance to rush.

The pains turned out to be the real thing and I had to stay. It took quite a while, and back then they used "twilight sleep" to make me super groggy and take away most of the pain. St. Mary's was a teaching hospital and it seemed to me that Dr. Forrester was talking and teaching during the birth.

I never saw or heard of Dr. Forrester again after I left the hospital. I heard that he had to go into the service. The Korean War had started by then.

Penni Alyce was born early 1952, three days before my twentieth

Part II

birthday. I had figured the birth should probably be in March but I really hadn't counted carefully. Penni weighed four pounds and twelve ounces at birth. I stayed seven days at the hospital and was babied and helped to get back on my feet. They even came once a day to bathe my stitches in warm water. That felt really good since the stitches were painful. They helped me to the bathroom and of course brought my meals and kept me furnished with fresh water.

We hadn't bought very much in advance for our expected child. It may have had something to do with the fact that Ken's brother and sister-in-law had lost their first baby in childbirth.

Since we had no supplies for the new baby, Ken had to go buy a few things. One was a bassinet with folding legs and wheels. That turned out to have been a good buy. We used it for all six of our children and loaned it out to relatives and friends, so it was probably used by at least ten babies.

Ken also got diapers and blankets. Although I don't remember exactly what else he bought we got by very well. Ken's Mom was a really good seamstress and soon there was at least one pretty dress for tiny Penni.

Along about this time Ken's Mom made me a pretty two-piece forest green, outfit. It was made of faille, which was a special shiny, sturdy fabric. The problem was I was kind of broad shouldered and she had not measured that. I really, really tried to wear that top but it was absolute misery. I could not manage to scrunch up enough for it to be comfortable.

I wanted to breastfeed but Penni was a slow eater so it was a little tricky. I went home after one week but Penni was supposed to weigh 5 pounds in order to go home, so she had to stay an extra two weeks plus. All the while Penni was in the hospital Ken took breast milk every day so she would have it there. (I still have the old-fashioned breast pump but the bulb has become rock hard.)

The waiting was hard. When she finally got to come home she was a little over three weeks old. She weighed 5 pounds 5 ounces. She was still a sluggish eater so we had to have good scales to weigh her before and after she fed so we would know if she was getting enough nourishment. There were to be no diaper changes until she was weighed. It was kind of awkward for we had to have a large pair of scales the baby could actually be laid on.

My Mom came and stayed a week with us when we brought Penni home. I don't know how she slept. She must have brought her own bedding and slept on the floor in the kitchen. Ken never volunteered to give up his bed. I'm sure she wouldn't have taken it anyway but I always felt bad for her.

This was an exciting time as well as a time of much learning. I had never babysat. (My brother, who was the youngest in our family, was a little over four years younger than me.) I had never changed a diaper and I had never really had to put someone else completely first in my thinking and actions. There was one thing that Dr. Forrester said, though, that made an impression on me. He said, "Don't forget you have a husband." I always tried to keep that in mind.

St. Mary's offered classes to teach new mothers how to care for their babies so of course I sat in on those. Also, the Visiting Nurses sent someone to check on things to make sure everything was going as it should after Penni came home.

Bath time was a bit of an ordeal, for it was in the dead of winter and the apartment was chilly. I tried to heat the kitchen by turning on the gas cook stove but that only helped a little. The table had to be cleared and baby blankets and towels placed on it for her to lie on. Then the small tub of warm water was set next to that. There I was, awkward anyway, trying to hurry and probably scaring Penni to death. She cried a lot during this process but from fright or discomfort, I was never really sure…maybe a little of both.

Ken took quite a few pictures of Penni during this time. She was cute and very small. The size suited me fine for I was thin and she was easy to hold. She did take a lot of time nursing for she was slow and I wanted to make sure she got all she could. There was one silly thing I did, but as I said I was just learning. I would check to see if she was wet even when she was sleeping. If she was even a little wet I would go ahead and change her, which upset her and made her cry. I used twelve dozen diapers a week. They all had to be washed and hung outside to dry. Once Ken tried to help hang them out to dry. I tried to tell him how to do it and he never tried to help with that job again.

There was a reasonable space in the backyard at the Pennsylvania Avenue address for hanging the laundry. We have pictures of Penni in the laundry basket as well as of her first time touching and sitting in the grass. We were always interested in her reaction to different things. She didn't have a big reaction to grass, but it was different for her.

It was along about this time that we first encountered the Bises. Since we had not been to church much because of going back to see our folks and then having little Penni, Lafayette Park Baptist Church sent someone to visit us. It was Lindell Bise who came. I think we had not yet met Anna. Lindell tried to tell us they could feed Penni in the nursery. We did not try to explain the problem with that. Later it was in Sunday School that I got to meet Anna and realized I very much wanted her for a friend. I think it was while we still lived at the Pennsylvania address that we started asking them over to have Sunday dinner with us.

Things were fairly calm for several months and seemed to be going pretty well. The landlady was having another baby. She already had several small children. She kind of went off the deep end and had to be hospitalized and have electroshock treatments. We heard that after the electroshock treatments she didn't remember her latest baby. I don't know if that was before or after an episode I experienced.

One day I could hear her in the hallway downstairs. She didn't sound right so I was holding Penni as she came upstairs. She was throwing pictures in frames down the stairs from where they hung on the walls. She wanted our doors open, so I just sat in a chair with Penni, trying to keep Penni quiet so the woman wouldn't decide to throw her down the stairs, too. It was a scary time.

We started looking for a new apartment right away.

Chapter 4

The next place we lived was at 1818 Rutger Street. Ken's brother, Wilber, and his family lived on the second floor in the front apartment and we lived in the apartment behind theirs. This place also had two rooms, furnished, and there was an alcove where we later put our washing machine.

It was our first Maytag washing machine and it was much appreciated. It would be over sixty years and a few other Maytags before I finally bought a different brand after Ken passed away.

Penni started learning to walk while we were living on Rutger Street. I never felt the floors were clean enough for her to be on the floor to learn to crawl so we would stand her on the floor where she could walk. If she fell we stood her on her feet again. We finally did have to let her down on the floor so she could learn to get herself up.

While Penni was pretty small we got our first new car. It was a 1953 Dodge. Ken's folks had moved back to the country after living in Salem for a few years. When we pulled into their driveway and were getting out of the car Ken's Mom rushed out and said, "Give me my baby." I replied, "She's not yours. She's mine." She responded, "Well, she's part mine." Recognizing the wisdom of her statement I handed Penni over. Another lesson learned.

It was nice to have family in the same apartment house. Wilbur and Wilma had two girls. Donna was about three years older than Penni and Sandra was about two or three months younger.

Part II

One time when Penni was about seven months old she had a crying spell and I could not find anything to make her feel better. Finally I patted her little leg and in a sort of crying voice I told her I had tried everything I knew to do and I just did not know how to help her. She looked at me solemnly and stopped crying. It was as if she understood what I was saying. I soon found she was cutting a tooth.

Penni was a thumb sucker. While sucking her right thumb she twisted her hair with her left hand. After a while she started getting a really thin spot where she twisted her hair. My Dad gave her a sort of boyish haircut and that helped a little. I think we had to work with her a little to get her to stop pulling or twisting her hair. When her hair did get a little longer it was a little curly and it was really pretty. Penni's hair was a light brown.

Soon Anna and Lindell Bise moved into the second floor in the rear of the building next door to us on Rutger Street. These seemed to be two buildings that shared a central wall. So it was nice having them living in the house next to us.

I thought it was interesting when one time she brought her seven-month-old son, Kendell, with her to visit. She had brought a toy for him and he was standing by the couch. Penni was a little older and she reached for the toy that was on the couch. Kenny, right away, let her know that was his toy. I had never seen a child with a sense of ownership so young.

Chapter 5

Wilma and Wilber were a few weeks ahead of us with the birth of their next baby, Michael. He was a regular size baby and things seemed okay. Ken's mom said several times through the years that it was so special that the kids were all okay.

In the summer of 1954, when Penni was about two and a half years old, we had our second baby, Karen. She weighed five pounds and fifteen ounces. She didn't have much hair but had a pretty face and was a pleasant baby from the start. There didn't seem to be any sibling rivalry and she was soon included without any problems. That summer was really hot. Karen seemed to have a little extra layer of skin so when she tried to sweat she got little water blisters on her skin. I would wipe her skin with a tissue and the tiny blisters would just wipe off.

Ken's sister had married the guy from the third floor on Nicholson place about a year and a half after we were married and they were also starting a family. Their baby, Dennis was a few months younger than Michael and Karen.

That summer we had a rain, hail, and wind storm. It was raining pretty heavily one Sunday but we went on to church. I think there was hail also while we were in the church parking lot. When we got home later in the evening we discovered a real mess. I think all the windows had been broken, shattered, and blown into the apartment on one side of the building. The only one not broken was the one in the back of the apartment. The broken glass was especially bad on the baby bed, which was next to a window. We had a lot of cleaning up to do before we could go to bed that night. Ken thought we still slept in the apartment that night since the storm was over and the night was still warm. It was probably in August or early September.

I think it was at about this time both sets of grandparents decided to give Penni a rocking chair. My parents gave her a nice wooden chair with turned spindles and Ken's parents gave her a platform rocker with green plastic upholstery. It turned out that with each new baby we would give the "old baby" a new baby doll to rock while I was feeding the new baby. I don't remember the doll, but it surely started with the new rocking chairs. It didn't take very long until both little rocking chairs were being used.

There are pictures of special toys the girls had but they must have broken from use, for they disappeared. We did not have space to keep extra things.

As in the other apartments, the bathroom was in the hallway and we shared it with Wilma's family. The laundry soon could be done in our apartment and again I hung it in the yard to dry. It was really nice that the coal burning furnaces were being phased out so there wasn't coal dust to fall on the laundry.

(I think we moved to St. Louis just after the big air clean up from the many years of coal-burning stoves and furnaces. There was still some evidence of a dirtier time but by 1950 and afterward the air was cleaner and we didn't get so much fall-out from coal smoke on the laundry when we hung it in the yard. I had heard something about the problem of the coal smoke and did notice some of the coal dust in the dirt of the yard.)

It was here that Penni first watched out for Karen. It was sort of a toss-up as to which to take down to the yard first, the girls or the laundry. I decided I would take the girls down first, with Karen in the walker. Then I would rush back upstairs to get the basket of laundry. It was a little scary but it worked. I didn't like leaving the girls alone in the yard but there did not seem to be another way of managing the situation.

Penni had been so easy to potty train that I expected the job to be an easy one with the others too. That turned out not to be the case and we did have to work at it.

One year we got Penni a really pretty new brown tweed winter coat trimmed in brown velvet. The first year it was actually too big for her, the next year it fit, and the year after that it was time to buy Karen a coat. Penni's coat was two years old but I just couldn't start a tradition of always putting Karen in the two-year-old coat. We bought Karen a new coat which wasn't quite as nice or pretty as Penni's had been but it was new and Penni wore her coat one more year.

At this apartment I started trying to branch out in my cooking. My first biscuits were small and hard! Ken pronounced them as just the way he liked them. (I really didn't believe him and thought he was just being gallant.) His Mom could make the best melt-in-your-mouth biscuits ever. He claimed that the soft ones were too soft and you couldn't even spread butter on them. Mine were so hard I couldn't even bite into them. I must have forgotten the baking powder.

Part II

Chapter 6

The Bise, Gleason and Edwards Families

During these years we started including the Bises' friends, the Gleasons, in our get-togethers. The Gleason's little son, Paul, was just a little older than Kenny Bise. We were all together quite a bit with our young growing families. About a year and a half after Karen was born we had Jeffrey. John was born after Jeff, and after we moved to Columbia, Illinois, Celia and Darla were born.

A Good While Back

By now with all these babies it is getting confusing to try to keep all of them in the proper sequence. Dorothy and Wilfred Gleason had Paul and Joy. Anna and Lindell had Kendall, VanDoyle, and Terri and Toni (twins). Wilber and Wilma had Donna, Sandra, Michael, and Sherri (and later, Randall and Richard). Naomia and Jackie had Dennis and Suzette (and later, Douglas).

I still had not learned to drive, but we had only one car anyway, and Ken used it to get to work. Through the union that Ken belonged to we had good medical coverage at what was called the Labor Health Institute or LHI. I decided one day to take the kids to the doctor. It was probably a check-up for Jeff. Not being able to drive, of course I needed to take the city bus. It stopped about a block from our apartment. I had Penni, about four and a half; Karen, a little younger than two; and Jeff, a few months old, a fairly large baby. As soon as I got on the bus and got the girls seated, the bus started to move. I grabbed a pole so I wouldn't fall and I squashed the hand of a frail looking little old lady sitting there. That shook me up a little, so for the ride home I called a taxi. It seemed like he took the long way around to get us home.

Penni and Karen had each nursed until they got their first tooth. They were only allowed one bite with the new tooth and then they went on the bottle. Jeff also started out breastfeeding. When he was about three months old, as I was feeding him strained beets he started breathing funny and sputtering red beets all over everything. (Don't ask about my feeding him vegetables at that age; I was trying to follow doctor's instructions.) We rushed him to the doctor. It turned out he had pneumonia and had to go to the hospital. I think he may have only been in Children's Hospital for three days, but with all the fuss and bother, my milk dried up, so he went on the bottle when we brought him home.

Ken had joined the church softball team, and after Jeff seemed to be okay we went to one of Ken's games. It was at this first game we went to that Ken slid into a base—second base I think—and broke both bones above the ankle in his lower right leg. He straightened the leg since it was turned sideways. When a teammate came to check on him, he asked Ken if he could wiggle his toes. He could, so the teammate pronounced the leg not broken. (Wrong!) Anyway, I guess someone took the family home and an ambulance took Ken to City Hospital. He spent the night there and the next day was transferred to Faith Hospital for surgery to stabilize the broken bones.

    I do not remember the logistics for visiting Ken in the hospital but I'm sure I was able to see him often. I also don't remember how long he had to stay in the hospital. They put him in a long cast that went from covering his whole foot almost all the way to his hip. After he was able to leave the hospital we didn't try to stay in the apartment on Rutger. We returned to Dent County and stayed with his folks, where I started learning to drive. The way Ken's Mom remembered it, there was a lot of crying. (Me not Ken)

    I was really tense driving and was the one who drove when Ken had to go back to St. Louis for the first check-up on his leg. I still wasn't holding my foot right on the gas pedal and that made driving hard. Then there was the fact that the highway seemed awfully narrow, especially meeting traffic. That would have been 1956.

    Ken's recovery took a while but finally, probably after the second cast, Ken was able to go back to work. He was still in a long cast but I think this one had a little heel.

    So we moved back to St. Louis.

Chapter 7

Moving back to St. Louis was another adventure. This time we found a little apartment on Hickory Street, which was the street parallel to Rutger Street. It didn't seem to be a part of town where we really wanted to live, so soon we found a nicer place on Geyer Avenue. I was still driving Ken to work. That was a bit of a challenge with young children. Ken put up with it; he was glad to get back to work. He was later put into a cast that was below the knee. I think it was called a walking cast and had a little heel. He was still working for Brown Shoe Company.

Ken worked in the warehouse where the upper leather was received from somewhere then shipped out to the shoe factories. Upper leather was the leather that was used for the upper part of the shoes that Brown Shoe Company made in their factories.

The apartment on Geyer was our first unfurnished apartment, and we had very little furniture. Wanting to be helpful, a cousin, David Land, gave us a couch he had in his basement. Since we really didn't have much furniture, Ken helped bring it home. That thing was big, faded blue, dirty, and smelled of mice. I hated it at first sight and smell. I took that thing apart, and took it out to the trash a few pieces at a time over several weeks until it was out of the house. I did learn a little something about how the old couch was put together and I later used that knowledge to upholster other things.

At about the same time Lorene gave us a rug. She said it was

Part II

better than nothing. It was so threadbare that there was almost nothing but the backing. Needless to say, that didn't stay either.

Someone from where Ken worked gave us a very dirty, probably antique, gas kitchen stove. I really liked the stove and tried to clean it up but was only partly successful.

You can see we really did have people trying to help. I guess it is the thought that counts.

While we lived at the Geyer Street address, all three kids got the measles at about the same time. By then Aunt Lennie had moved to a place on Mississippi Avenue just around the corner from where we lived. She came over quite a lot to help rock and comfort the little ones. That was very special help.

Jeff was still very much a baby while we lived on Geyer. We were still using glass baby bottles; plastic bottles hadn't yet been invented. When Jeff had all he wanted from his bottle he liked to stand by the bed rail, hold the bottle by the nipple over the floor, then drop it. We cleaned up broken glass and spilled milk from several bottles.

Our apartment was on the second floor, directly above the Linch family. Mrs. Linch was our landlady. Jeff liked to run across the wooden floor in his large, heavy walker, and that worried me. I didn't want to aggravate the landlady. We liked this place. They never complained to us about the noise, however.

A couple of things happened in that apartment that were probably noteworthy. We had a pretty red step stool. The kids were allowed to sit on the stool but were told not to push with their feet against a nearby shelf. I thought Karen pushed and the stool turned over with her. I was so upset and scared I picked her up and spanked her. Much later she told me she felt that was very unfair since she was reaching for a towel to help, not pushing on the shelf.

Penni remembers sweeping the very steep stairs that led down to the back yard, falling and getting hurt with several scrapes and cuts.

Jeff used the walker in the house but I would not let the kids ride the tricycle in the house. Karen said later I had not said she couldn't ride the tricycle in the yard so one time when we were still napping

A Good While Back

she tried to take it outside down the very steep stairs. She said there was a string across the top of the stairs, probably as a notice that the kids were not to go down alone. She decided to use the string to let the tricycle down the stairs. The problem was she didn't know how to tie a knot. The tricycle got down on it's own. Apparently it made such a clatter that Mrs. Linch and I both showed up…and she still didn't get to ride it, even in the yard.

Mom tried to help by sending clothes for the kids. They were light weight and not very warm for Karen. I picked her up in the yard late one day while I was visiting with Mrs. Linch. It was getting cool and I was hugging her pretty tightly trying to keep us both warm and I started to shiver. Karen said, "Mommy you rattle."

Part II

Chapter 8

Aunt Lennie had come from her apartment around the corner on Mississippi Avenue and helped rock the kids when they were sick. So when it was getting time for the next baby to be born, she felt free to make suggestions for names. We had sort of picked out Gregory John but Aunt Lennie said we were about to run out of John Edwards. When the baby turned out to be a boy we decided to name him John Gregory. The really funny part of that was Aunt Lennie was married to (and widowed from) John Smith. Their son was John Dallas, their grandson was named John Douglas and later the next generation was John D____ (something). I guess they really liked the name John.

Stores had plastic bags for things, so I used one of those to cover John's diapers. Plastic pants and liners were just becoming available about then. What a breakthrough! Without them you could really get wet when a baby wet its diaper while you were holding him. I never minded changing diapers. It was just part of the process. We used a diaper pail with borax water to soak the diapers in. They came out nice and white with regular laundering.

Penni started kindergarten in St. Louis and walked to school alone most of the time. I have forgotten the name of the school but it was very close and she attended there until she finished first grade. That was in the middle of the term elsewhere so she had to repeat the last half of the year when we moved to Columbia, and finish in the spring. It made her older in her class, but it might have helped her be more mature in her class.

I first started canning fruit for the family while we lived at the Geyer Street address. Someone gave us quite a bit of fruit. I think it was pears. I had watched Mom do canning and had helped when I was needed and asked. Early on I got an instruction book titled *Ball's Blue Book*. It gave instructions on canning and drying various types of produce. It has been a great help through the years. The extra food always came in handy with a growing family.

We were still friends with the Bises and Gleasons when we moved back to St. Louis. Of course it would happen that when Anna was pregnant with twins and I was having a baby shower for her at the Geyer apartment, she went into labor. We notified Lindell, who was at work, and Ken took her to the hospital, where Lindell met them.

We finished the shower without Anna, but it put a bit of a damper on the party.

PART II

CHAPTER 9

Less than a year after John was born we moved to Columbia, Illinois. Jackie Asbridge (Naomia's husband) knew people in Columbia who wanted to sell their house, so after we checked on it we got a loan from Mom and Dad and bought the house.

The house really wasn't much. A neighbor, Mr. Probstmeier seemed to enjoy telling us it had been a barn that was turned into a house. It had a basement, first floor and a second floor. It had two rooms on the second floor and two rooms and a bathroom on the first floor. There was an extra half-bath in the basement. The half bath flushed up to the sewer system. The basement drain came out under the driveway and down the hill.

The thing that made the property special was the large yard with a few trees. The place had an extra lot on the side, which was a rather steep hill. Actually the extra lots were sort of on the end of a rounded end of a ridge and tapered down to a small drainage ditch.

I could tell that when Mom first saw the house she was very disappointed. It had the old-fashioned tan-brick-look tar paper siding. But, it was our place and we would find room for everyone.

The heating unit for the little house was a floor furnace that got really hot. One time Penni stumbled and fell onto it. She got a pretty bad burn with hatch marks on her arm from the grate. After we did an add-on to the house we put in a whole house furnace, and that was a lot better.

A Good While Back

The two rooms upstairs were bedrooms. The first floor had a tiny living room and kitchen toward the front of the house with the bathroom behind the living room. The stairways up and down were sort of behind and beside the kitchen. We borrowed money from Ken's folks and before the year was out Ken and my Dad added two larger rooms to the back of the little house.

Soon after we moved into the house in Columbia we discovered Jeffrey was having trouble hearing. I had asked him to go get something for me and while he was practically standing on my toes looking up at my face, trying to understand what I was saying, John, who was two years younger, ran and got it. We had really good medical coverage through Ken's labor union so I got Jeff to the doctor right away. He needed tubes in his ears to drain fluid from behind the eardrums.

It was so special having good doctors available that we got things taken care of right away once we recognized a problem. Part of the help was a nurse at the LHI who could advise so I knew whether to take the child to the doctor. Her name was Maria Rothfischer. I mentioned it later to a friend and she had also been helped by this special nurse.

PART II

CHAPTER 10

We were used to going to church so we looked up the First Baptist Church right away. That was either November or December of 1958. It was in a storefront on Main Street. John was less than a year old and we noticed another little boy just a little older. He was a member of the Halleran family.

We joined that church and soon started getting involved in their various activities. We stayed involved for several years.

Having the new addition on the house gave us a large eat-in kitchen. Mom and Dad had given us a nice sturdy wooden table. To make room for eight at our table, Ken made a sturdy wooden bench for one side. On the other side of the table there was room for two chairs and the high chair sort of at the corner. Ken and I sat at the ends of the table.

The new kitchen had a nice group of cabinets for storage. One of the special things was there were enough drawers for the (eventually six) kids to each have a drawer where they could store special things. Another thing I thought was interesting was when the older kids cleaned out their drawers they let the younger ones have anything from the things they were discarding. There really was not much to throw away.

The basement was never fully dug out under the new section of the house, and the basement walls were concrete block. One of the things I remember about the beginning of the digging process was little John with black dirt on his face. He had obviously tasted it. The basement space was used to store tools. Later it had shelves to hold the canning from the garden produce.

Something else that Ken did was break a round hole through the basement wall in the old part of the house to have access to the new part. That was very helpful.

The new part of the house also let us have a good size living room. We later added a fitted set of bookshelves there. I think the ceiling slanted a little on the sides.

Ken made changes to the upstairs so that the rooms had separate doors from the stairs. That way we could have a girls' room and a boys' room. He also put a closet in the boys' room. There was already a closet in the girls' room.

Ken made bunk beds for the girls. We had purchased bunk beds for the boys. The boys' beds were not as stable as the girls' beds so one time when John, on the lower bunk, was pushing up with his feet it caused the upper bunk to fall onto him. They did not tell me until much later.

I'm not sure of the exact sequence of events but at some point the boys' bunk bed was replaced with a larger, heavier bunk bed. This time it was Jeff, pushing with his feet who got that upper bunk dumped on him.

We turned the downstairs room that had been the living room into our bedroom and Ken added a closet and a sliding door between the two sections. We still had the old front door in our bedroom and the small front porch just outside.

PART II

Olieta and Kenneth
Karen, Jeff
John, Penni, Celia,
Darla in 1964

While Darla was still in the baby bed we realized she had severely turned-in feet. With the good medical treatment available, she was put into heavy-duty baby shoes with a metal brace attached to the shoes, which she wore mostly at night. This brace was adjusted gradually over time to cause her feet to turn to a more natural direction. It did not seem to bother her at all. She still stood in her bed. When she turned over while sleeping she would make a noisy KLUNK. That just meant the brace was doing its job.

Living in our house in Columbia turned out to be much better than living in St. Louis. The first year we were there I made the children's first sled. Money was tight for us; Ken kept a tight budget and we couldn't just go out and buy a sled. It was rather difficult to make, but since we had a very nice little hill even the heavy wooden sled with its hemp rope was used for many years. When we could finally afford to purchase a sled, they still used the old sled, too. There never seemed to be any problem with sharing.

It was so satisfying to finally have a good place for the kids to play. At one point we had a sand box. We did finally have to make a lid for it because neighbor cats wanted to use the sand box for a litter box.

We got our first dog after we moved to Illinois. It was a little mutt that we got from acquaintances. It was small and kind of cute. He was black with brown and white markings and had little floppy ears. We named him Wags. We weren't into training puppies and at that time dogs lived outside. Once when Celia was just big enough to run I noticed little Wags chasing little Celia, and Celia seemed to be a little scared. It was so cute the two little beings together in the yard.

I also made the kids' first swing. It was an old-fashioned rope and board swing. The first seat just had a notch cut into each end of the wooden board to help hold it to the rope. That turned out to be not quite satisfactory because of the many times the seat had to be put back onto the rope. At some point Ken took the swing down, fixed a new board with holes for the rope and rehung it.

One tree had the swing and it eventually became a really special place for the kids for many years. Even years later when I was babysitting Darla's kids I would see little Kenny laying across the wooden seat of the swing on a cold winter day gently swaying back and forth.

One summer the kids decided they didn't have anything to do

and came to me with that complaint. I was feeling silly and jokingly said, "Oh, go climb a tree." Penni said, "Can we? Oh, can we?" and they rushed out to the largest of the little trees in the back yard. Penni and Karen could both climb the tree. Jeff was three or four years old and cried to climb it, too. They helped him up to the first limb and on to the tree. Then he was stuck. He couldn't get up or down. We had to make a new rule: They had to be able to climb the tree by themselves and get down by themselves.

Karen was in about second grade when she came home one day and asked to take a comic book to school the next day. I asked her why she wanted to do that and she told me she didn't have enough to do. She didn't just like to read the comics; she also studied how they were drawn. I talked to her teacher and she was able to find something more challenging for Karen. Karen did not make that request again. I think they had a special class for more advanced students and she ended up in one of those a little later. At one point she was in a half and half class with third graders.

Our kids never had a play set but they had the tree. And we never had a broken bone from falls from that tree. Even the neighbor boys climbed the tree with our boys and never had a problem. I still have a picture of the climbing tree full of not-so-little boys.

At some point when Karen was pretty small she climbed up in the tree to see bird eggs in a nest. The mother bird came back to the nest while Karen was up there. It was a real thrill that she could be so quiet the bird would come back.

One day Jeff decided to climb a dead tree down the hill and fell when a limb broke. Penni said Jeff wasn't breathing after he fell. She carried him partway up the hill before he started breathing again. Jeff later said he got the idea to climb the tree from the oldest of the boys next door.

Once when Karen was having some kind of trouble we took her to the doctor. I still don't remember what the diagnosis was, or even if he gave us one, but he prescribed a bicycle for her. She was number two of five at the time. She must have been close to nine years old and the bicycle had to be a small one. It was not easy riding the thing on soft grass, and we had a very short driveway, but Karen and Jeff learned to ride it anyway.

One day Karen let Jeff ride the bike to school. As John was leaving kindergarten to walk home (we were about one-half mile from school) he saw the bicycle in the bike rack outside school. I guess he thought it should not be there so he pushed it home because he still could not ride it. He looked so innocent pushing that thing home that I just could not punish him for it. But he did have to push the bike back to school so Jeff wouldn't panic, thinking it had been stolen. It was just too awkward to get Celia ready to go and take her along so he had to do it by himself.

It is going to be hard to remember and tell much of what was going on during our thirty-six or so years at that place. John was almost a year old when we moved there in the early winter of 1958. Our wooden table was just the right height for John to duck under the edge and stand up under it. After he had played under the table for a while he would decide it was time to get out. He nearly always ducked down to miss the edge of the table, misjudged and came up directly under the place he was trying to avoid.

There was a time John had a problem while we were visiting Ken's folks in the country. The house had a small, under-the-eves upstairs where the grandkids slept. One of those collapsible child gates was placed at the head of the stairs. John was trying to open the gate when he lost his balance and fell down the stairs. I think the back of his little head hit every bare, oak step all the way down. That was scary.

Penni was probably in third grade when she offered to help a classmate with some of the lessons. I heard later that when his mother tried to tease him about having a girlfriend he replied, "She's not a girl, she's Penni."

One time in grade school Darla befriended a new girl. I think her name was Jill. Darla helped her get adjusted to the new school and her new situation. While they never became best buds, Jill came to her later and thanked her for being a special help. Darla always had a soft spot for the older ladies in the neighborhood and helped out when she could. She bought cigarettes for Mrs. Alexander. She visited with Mrs. Winnel in the new apartments. Mrs. McDonald was looking for someone to weed her flower beds and help with housework so Darla applied for the job. She was probably twelve or so and had to have a trial period to prove she could do the job. After she got the job and was finished each time, they would share cookies and lemonade and visit.

Chapter 11

We had our first garden the spring after we moved to Columbia. It was at the top of the hill just a little way behind the house. Ken made a plan even for that first garden. I do not remember when he began buying books on gardening but that little garden was very precise. I remember we planted peas but I do not remember what else. One of the early years it had snowed after the little garden was planted and I looked out and saw two of the neighbor kids walking very carefully down one of the rows that was perfectly outlined by the light snow. I was very upset and yelled out the door at them. I felt bad right away about the yelling but I did not know how to undo it.

Mr. Probstmeier had a garden just a few feet from ours and just over the top of the hill. He grew strawberries there. Our children would watch him pick the berries and occasionally he would give them some.

We eventually bought the back side of the hill. Ken terraced it, which made several flat places that made plowing and planting easier. One of the easier things we grew there was potatoes. I think Ken did most of the work but several of us would help at various times, especially at harvest time. Ken worked on the soil to make it rich and loose, which made digging and gathering the potatoes a lot easier.

A family named Heck owned the place next door for a while.

Part II

Mr. Heck did not like our old woven wire fence on the back side of the hill and wanted us to take it out. It did not seem like a good idea to us so we left it in place. He was so upset with it he would ram it with his tiller when he was plowing his own garden.

The side lot and the back lot were sort of at the end of a ridge that went down to a small ditch with running water. I guess it was a sort of drainage ditch and of course through the years the kids had to play in the water. We later bought a partial lot across the little ditch and next to Mr. Probstmeier's house lot. We have remembered a few things from the last lot we bought from Mr. Probstmeier over by the curve and across from the cemetery at the end of North Saint Paul Street.

One of the things that happened over there was that when Ken was finishing mowing at dusk one evening he stepped into a yellow jacket's nest and got stung pretty badly.

Another thing that happened was when corn that was planted in the lower part of that space was almost ready to pick, we decided to wait one more day to pick it. Bad move! The raccoons got into the patch that night and ruined the whole crop. It was not that they ate all the sweet corn. They tore down stalks and tore into the nice corn ears and messed them up so they were not salvageable in any form.

Twice young drivers took the curve too fast and their cars landed in the upper part of that lot. The lightweight old fence did nothing to stop them. They never bothered us with it and managed to get their own help to get their cars out.

A few times our kids left home and then came back. John went the farthest. I think he had been to Texas and California.

Ken had put in a little Tulip tree at the corner of our property that was near the cemetery. That area became our dog cemetery. Wags and Matthew were both buried there.

Did I tell you about Matthew, a black Cocker Spaniel whose coat had red glints in the sun? He was one of our two hand-me-down or left-behind dogs. He originally belonged to John but when John left he did not take Matthew with him. The other dog was a small gray Schnauzer named Wendell. Wendell had been Karen's.

We planted a few trees over the years and later took some of them out. Of the original trees, the only tree we actually took out was an old one that grew beside the back corner of the house. I do not remember for sure what it was; it may have been a plum tree. I do remember that on that tree one cold windy day I saw a fairly large crested woodpecker. I never saw one of them again.

There was a white Peony bush and a few small rose bushes with beautiful bright red roses in the back yard of that old house. I could not keep the rose bushes alive. I guess they got aphids and I didn't know about spraying for the little bugs. We planted a pink Peony bush that turned out to be very pretty and we enjoyed it very much.

Some blue irises grew on the little bank between our place and the next place up the hill. I put in a few more that were larger and different colors. I always enjoyed the iris blooms and the fact that there were usually more than one bloom on each stalk. I took a few bulbs with me when we moved to Temple Street.

One of the trees I especially enjoyed was a redbud tree Ken put in at the very top of the hill. In the early spring when it was in full bloom and the new grass was at it's brightest after a rain and the sky was bright blue it was a scene of the purest beauty.

We also put in a few fruit trees but they never grew to be very productive. I also tried growing herbs but I never got very good at using them, probably because I didn't plan ahead well enough to have them ready when they were needed in a dish.

Another tree that I found interesting on that place was a wild cherry not far from the redbud tree and the climbing tree. It was also near where our first garden had been. One year during a storm the top broke off the tree. It left a large limb sticking out pretty far from the trunk. That limb sent out a small upright limb, which eventually formed a new kind of top. The white blooms in the spring were pretty.

The grass was really soft and green at that old place. Ken tried to keep it pretty and mowed. With the shape of the property, mowing was not an easy job. After a few years Ken's knees started to bother him and before we moved from there he eventually had to have knee-replacement surgery for both knees.

One year some group in the county was giving away pine tree seedlings. I only wanted one but took the twenty-five they were offering. Ken planted them just beyond the climbing tree. As they grew they created quite a little forest and were really very pretty. But I think they were the first things to go when we finally sold the old house.

Chapter 12

Another of the special things we had early on at the Saint Paul address was Ken's new dark room. It took up most of one side of the small basement. There was already water there with the pipes from the old kitchen and the half-bath in what was really the front corner of the house.

He started his own business and called it KCE Studio. He did a good little bit of business and his pictures were very good. Much of the business was from First Baptist Church of Columbia. He took quite a few pictures of special events, especially progress in getting upgrades to the space for worship. There were also pictures of the new pastor and deacons.

Along with this, Ken had church jobs such as song leader, janitor, and deacon.

I had a job, mostly in the nursery but I also later led the Acteens. The two things that stand out in my mind about that job were a sleepover at church. It was really miserable for me because I was so sleepy but the girls seemed to enjoy the activity. I would turn the lights out and the girls would turn them back on. Then I remembered where the fuse box was since Ken was working as janitor. The girls did not know where the fuse box was. Problem solved.

The other thing for the girls was a book study on Alaska. I had worked really hard on the book study. We had it at our house and had refreshments. I was so thrilled that the girls again seemed to have a good time and maybe actually learned something important.

When the kids came in from school I would be working in the kitchen and I would ask how their day was. The boys would say, "fine" and head on upstairs. The girls would usually stop and talk a little while.

Sometimes kids do things at an early age that make you wonder what they will turn out to be.

Jeff drew a picture of a tree at an early age. A lot of kids draw a tree standing on top of the ground. Jeff's tree had roots. He did turn out to have a more scientific mind than some of the others.

When we got our own television, it was positioned so it could be seen from the kitchen. Ken liked to watch television while we ate supper and his chair was positioned for him to do that. Karen liked to talk at the supper table, so once I tried to limit her to telling about her day in three sentences. It was very hard for her. She later told me it was really mean. But she actually missed her desert one time because of her inattention to the meal while she was talking.

I mentioned earlier that when Mom married Dad she had to give up her piano. I had many times had the urge to try to play the piano at Aunt Laura's house. When I noticed the same tendencies in Penni, I wanted a piano. Jackie Asbridge knew of what seemed to be an abandoned house near where they lived at the time and offered to bring a piano from there to us.

The piano was old and very much out of tune. We could not afford to have it tuned, and did not know much about such things anyway. The young man who was helping with the music at church was willing to give Penni piano lessons when we asked. She readily took to the piano. When Penni was ten years old she played the piano for Vacation Bible School. Some lady at church had commented that Penni would not be able to do that because her hands were too small. Penni proved her wrong. She did play for Vacation

Bible School that year and even played a special anthem…and did it beautifully.

A couple of years later we started Karen on the piano. She also did well and several years later the girls were playing the piano and organ at church. As with our piano at home, the piano at church was badly out of tune. It was so old it could not be tuned completely and to make it work with the little organ, Penni had to raise everything a half step and Karen had to lower everything a half step. I always enjoyed hearing them play together.

A couple of years after Karen started taking piano lessons we started Jeffrey with lessons. It was harder to get him to practice. One time we took a picture of him at the piano and he looked so sad and dejected that we let him quit. It just wasn't worth the pain.

Penni tried the saxophone since that was what was available to borrow from the school, but she hated it. It was heavy to lug back and forth to school and Karen sometimes tried to help carry the thing. Anyway, Penni could not have disliked the saxophone any more than I did. It was the most awful screechy thing I ever heard. Of course she was just beginning to try to learn how to play, but I felt I could not adjust to listening to the practice. The band leader wanted her to try the tympani drums but she felt she didn't have a good enough ear for it. Karen says after Penni's bad experience, we didn't let her try a band instrument.

Jeffrey was later able to join the school band and play the slide trombone that belonged to the school. John played the French horn in the band, also a school instrument. They brought their instruments home to practice. Ken had taken a course to learn to make cases. He made cases to fit the school instruments that Jeff and John learned to play because their cases were in need of replacing. Ken's cases did not contour to fit like the original but had lines that slanted to meet the needs.

Among the instruments Celia tried was an old wooden clarinet borrowed from cousin Suzy, as well as tympani and bassoon borrowed from the school. These did not take with her although she did bring home pads and drum sticks to practice with. Darla played the slide trombone that Jeff had played and it still had its case with the straight lines that Ken had made.

I could stand hearing the girls practice some of their songs over and over on the piano, but Ken had trouble listening to the same songs over and over through the years so I would try to schedule practice before he came home from work. The reason it seemed so repetitive was because the girls used some of the same piano books.

Eventually Celia played for churches of different denominations during her marriage to a man in the Army. Darla had piano lessons too but they did not seem to take for her.

Penni and Karen both continued playing the piano. Penni studied organ in college and I think both played for their churches at times. Some of the grandkids also played music, and when they were old enough we would have family concerts at our twice-yearly get-togethers. I have always attributed the music bent to Mom being the first influence in our family.

L-R: Kenneth, Olieta, John, Celia,
Penni, Darla (front), Karen, Jeff

Chapter 13

We did do some special things while the kids were young. A few times we camped out in state parks in Missouri. One time we went to Sam Baker State Park. We had a big old station wagon with extra seats added to the back so there were actually eight seats. We put all the camping gear, suitcases and everything else we thought we would need on the rack on the top of the station wagon. These trips were all with an older car with recapped tires. We did not have a bit of trouble, but thinking back it seems a little scary.

Sam Baker Park had big boulders and icy water. I may be mixing up the parks but I think that the park had paths between high bluffs. Cooking breakfast on the little raised cooking station was a bit of a challenge. We always had bacon and eggs for breakfast, so of course there was spattering bacon grease. The smoke followed me no matter on which side of the fire I stood. I assume it had something to do with wind currents and that my standing there changed the pattern no matter where I stood.

We always had a tent or two but that turned out not to be the only thing we had to cope with. Sleeping was a problem for me. The first time we went camping we had sleeping bags. Although we had checked the surface, there was a rock under my sleeping bag and I could not seem to get rid of it all night. I discovered the next morning that it was actually embedded in the dirt. Later we had canvas cots with the wood pieces on the sides. I had bony

Part II

knees anyway and when I turned onto my side I always bumped that wood. The canvas was really not enough padding to soften the feeling of the wooden sides of the cot.

We went to several of the state parks during those early years but I do not remember which ones they were.

A couple of years we camped on the farm we had been given by Ken's parents near where they lived. Once it rained and the tent was old and leaky. Some of us opted to stay and just stay out of the way of the drips. Others went back to Grandma and Grandpa's to finish the night.

Another time we spent the night in the old house on the farm. We spent some time trying to clean it but it had been used as storage and as a granary and was very dusty.

That house had originally been built as a living space for an aunt of Ken's who had fallen on hard times and needed a place to live with her several young children.

It had two rooms and a tiny attic. It was a bare-bones place on the order of the house I had lived in as a child, only smaller and we could hear strange noises under the house at night. I do not remember what we did for cooking.

That property had eighty acres with a nice open field in the back where someone had started a flat type of cactus that had pretty yellow blooms. The cactus had spread quite a bit into that back field. We learned later that there were a couple of apple trees over by the road. There were also several large oak trees between the little house and the road.

We could never see our way clear to move onto that property. By the time we retired it had become overgrown by red cedars and needed major work to restore it to the pretty open space that had been so attractive years before. By that time we were also more used to having people nearby and this place was pretty far out in the country. It was fairly close to a highway but still seemed isolated.

During the years on Saint Paul Street, Ken also dug out a flat place below the garage for an ice rink. I think the Smith children had moved away by then and the kids did not have many friends over. The idea really did not work out well for the rink was never used much. Ken even put up a light on a pole so they could skate at night, but even that improvement did not seem to help.

Next to the street was a mulberry tree. We were not used to that kind of berry so I never used them. I did not use the berries from some tall bushes, either. Some acquaintances used the mulberries as well as other berries. Of course they could have all they wanted of both of them. I guess I only wanted to use the things I knew about.

A gooseberry bush grew down beside the ditch and near the little culvert. When the bush finally got to be a pretty good size I picked the berries and made a pie. Ken liked gooseberries. These berries were not really a favorite of mine so I may have only used them once.

Later we found tiny wild strawberries on that place over near the fence on the east side of the property. We had to try a few of those. They were pretty but they were really sour.

Ken was really in his element with the gardening. Using the several gardening books he bought during the years, and several catalogs, he made diagrams of where the rows should be.

We grew potatoes, tomatoes, cucumbers, green beans, strawberries and other things. Most of the time the kids did not want to help in the garden; it was Jeff who would try to help even if it was cold and damp. We enjoyed the potatoes and canned a good bit of the other things. I made sweet pickles and dill pickles. I even tried sauerkraut at least once.

Some of those things were more work than others.

My very favorite thing was the thornless red ever-bearing raspberries. They did not bear very well but over time had quite a few berries. I said I knew we were rich when we could have fruit for breakfast.

Some people a few blocks away had a pear tree with pears that were not being used and they let us pick them. Generally they were not very tasty but with a little sugar added as we canned them they were a nice addition to our diet. They were very much appreciated.

Since we were just one-half mile from school the kids walked to and from school on their own. One time when Penni was pretty young, she was scared by a big dog barking at her while she was walking home alone. A neighbor two houses up from us, Mr. Bess, walked her safely the rest of the way home.

Another time, while Karen and Jeff were walking home, a larger boy pushed them down and climbed on their backs as though they were horses. I called his mother and we had no more trouble.

One mother sent over some used blue jeans. I guess she thought we were poor. Those jeans were huge and our boys were never able to wear them. Their ages may have been fairly close but the family must have been very large people.

The kids always had school pictures and we saved at least one of each of those for our photo collection. One thing I noticed about those pictures was that the kids looked so clean they just shined. Ken's mom made pretty gingham shirts for the boys and pretty dresses for the girls so they all looked really nice.

We did our own painting. When we painted the rooms I got to do the detail part. Ken painted the outside of the window frames in the new section but he was not careful, thinking it would be easy to scrape off the extra paint with a razor blade. I was the one to do the scraping and besides being hard to do it was also hard to reach the window frames that were very close to the old garage roof.

One time we were going to paint the little back porch. Penni wanted to do the job and was old enough to do it. The problem was that she had on a pretty new white blouse and failed to change out of it. Of course she got some silver gray splatters on it. It looked pretty tacky so to remedy the situation we used colored fabric paint and randomly put numbers and equations all over the thing. I guess we were ahead of the time for no one seemed to notice. At about the same time, Penni had a pair of tennis shoes that we tried to make last a little longer by sewing bright colored buttons on them.

I mostly enjoyed that place for there were large trees that shaded the house and helped keep it cool. We did buy an air conditioner for the living room after several years.

Chapter 14

As the kids grew a little older they did not always have their homework done by the time Ken said they had to go to bed. They would want me to call them a little early the next morning so they could finish it. I made little round clock faces with moveable hands from poster board. Then, in descending order age wise, I mounted the six on a piece of narrow ribbon and hung that on the unfinished doorframe between the old and new parts of the house.

The kids could then set their "clocks" for the time they wanted me to wake them up before school. Even before Darla was in school she would set her "clock" so she could be called at a certain time. This was one of the silly but very successful things we used during the early years. In recent years, with my children all fifty years old or more, I cut the ribbon and gave each their special "clock."

It actually may have meant more to me than to them.

The kids did sometimes get dirty around the place. Sometimes they liked to play in what we called the dirt basement. The basement was never completely cleared of the dirt lumps, and it did not have a concrete floor. We have pictures of very dirty little John and little Celia after they had been playing down there.

A special treat for the kids, and later Ken, was scraping the bowl after I had made a cake or cookies.

We have a special picture of Celia after she had a turn at the cake batter bowl. She never seemed to appreciate those pictures but they showed something of our family life back then.

Sometimes I had trouble getting things ready ahead of time. One of those was having the cookies ready for school lunches. Sometimes the kids would have to wait a few minutes so they could take a still-warm cookie to school along with their sandwich. Then they would have to rush to make it to school on time. I also tried to make sure the kids had apples in their lunches. I felt we could not afford an apple a day for me but I tried to make sure they each had one. I never thought to make sure the apples were tasty, but that was just the way it was. Many, many years later I learned that John would trade his apple for cookies.

There was another thing I did that had the "kids" wondering in later years. On a major shopping day after the latest payday I would buy one large candy bar and cut it into six pieces when I got home. Later they thought that was funny. The thing was…I wanted a candy bar but since money was tight they got the candy bar and I got the crumbs.

Chapter 15

We went to Salem periodically to see our parents, and since the two sets lived fairly close to each other we tried to divide our time between them.

One weekend after we had been down to see Mom and Dad, Dad telephoned saying Mom was sitting in her chair, needing to go to the bathroom and couldn't get up.

We went back to try to figure out what was going on and see how we could help. She was having a stroke.

Mom was seventy-eight years old and had seemed to be in fairly good health. She did have high blood pressure and her doctor had discontinued her blood pressure medicine.

After the stroke I kept thinking she was getting a little better as the days passed. I always have to learn things the hard way. I did not know I should have contacted her doctor to try to find out why he had discontinued her medicine.

I think Mom had blockage of one or both of her carotid arteries. The doctor explained that even if they did surgery there was no guarantee that she would wake up. We did not opt for the surgery.

Mom lasted thirteen days and people were coming and going, visiting her. Don came in from California but I do not remember seeing much of Oneta. I learned later she was kind of on the outs with Dad.

At her funeral Dad was so distraught he could not walk and was sort of dragged past the casket. All the while he was crying loudly and seemed to be almost at the point of collapse.

The funeral procession was the longest I had ever seen…but I had not been to many funerals. Mom had brothers and sisters still living, and several of them managed to be at the funeral.

I had not called all of her brothers and sisters when she suffered the stroke. At the funeral one of her brothers asked why we did not call. It was because I kept trying to think she was getting better.

Dad had thought that it was probably better that Mom died first because she couldn't drive a car. Wrong! He was so lonely he just couldn't stand it. He moved into a senior apartment complex in town and began doing somewhat better since he was around other people.

Soon Dad met an elderly lady, Zelma, and they became an item. One day a neighbor came up through the trap door from the basement to the kitchen as if trying to catch the old people in something.

When Dad decided to auction the household goods, people were in and out of Dad's house. Later I discovered a special piece of Mom's jewelry was missing. I suspected a cousin of taking it and justifying her actions by thinking Mom would have wanted her to have it.

I had wanted a special old fluted carnival glass bowl but Dad insisted I wait for the auction. He had given me $5,000 and I had used it for a down payment on a new little Buick Skyhawk. I planned to drive down and attend the auction. Ken told me not to buy more than would fit into that little car. Well, the bunk beds we had didn't necessarily seem appropriate for our now adult children. Getting into the spirit of the auction I bought two three-piece bedroom sets, several quilts, the carnival glass bowl for thirty dollars, and I'm not sure what else.

Ken was really not pleased with me and would not help me figure out how to get the beds home. His brother-in-law had an old pick-up truck and I asked to borrow it. Ken did go down to Salem in the car to help load things on the truck.

A Good While Back

I drove the Asbridges old yellow truck down those two lane roads on the way to Salem. The heavy old thing had a partially rusted out floor and I could see the road under my feet. On one stretch I was meeting a long string of cars when one driver decided to pull out to pass. I pulled over to the edge of the highway as far as I dared and kept going. Someone let that driver back in line and there was no real trouble.

We got to Salem, loaded the old truck, and covered the load with a tarp. Before we got all the way home it turned dark and the tarp came partially loose, flopping noisily the rest of the way home.

We probably waited until the next day to unload. Ken insisted the mattresses and springs would not fit through the door as we tried to take them up the stairs. They did fit, though, and we got them up the stairs without much room to spare…and without scraping anything.

Then there was another problem. Ken had made a really nice set of bunk beds for the girls and the new bed would not fit in the room with the bunk beds. Reluctantly I took the set of bunk beds apart and carried the pieces downstairs. Then one bedroom set with a double bed could go in the girls' room and the other could go into the boys' room. The smaller bunk bed set went into the bedroom downstairs for the youngest girls and everyone had a bed. I don't remember the exact timing of the different bed switches.

PART II

CHAPTER 16

I did a lot of sewing while the kids were growing up. I think it was mostly boys' shirts, Ken's shirts, and dresses for me. In the Baptist Church at that time there was no dancing. So when it was prom time it was decided to have something special for the teenagers at church. Penni needed a special dress.

For the dress she chose a heavyweight satin in white for the top and pink for the skirt. The entire dress was to be covered with pink Chantilly lace that had a pretty rose pattern. The lace came in a much more narrow fabric and had to be figured differently from the wider fabric we usually got. The satin was not a problem. The problem came when I tried to match the pattern at the seams of the narrow lace. The dress pattern was gored with seams across the breasts vertically and similar seams in the skirt. I got the seams with the two halves of the flowers matching on the front of the dress. I held my breath as I waited to see how well the pattern matched on the back of the dress. When they matched on the back of the dress as well I think we were all thrilled.

A year or two later I made a dress for Karen. She chose fabrics that were easier to sew. It may have been at my suggestion. Karen's dress was an easier satin and was blue with a chiffon overskirt. It was very pretty on her.

A little later I made Penni's wedding dress. It was white crepe with lace trim. She came home most weekends to supervise every

A Good While Back

step of the process. It turned out very well, too, and their wedding pictures were special.

The purpose of this story was to show our "kids" and grandkids, something of what it was like growing up at the time Ken and I did, as well as later. It seems to be almost a life story. I wanted to show them a glimpse of a time when things were not so readily available to buy cheaply. We learned to be self-sufficient and frugal because that's what was necessary in those times. We survived with commitment, self-sacrifice and forward thinking.

Time marched on and each of the kids finished high school and went on to do their own things.

Back: Jeff, John
Front: Penni, Darla, Celia, Karen

Part II

Chapter 17

One of the special things I got to do while we lived on North Saint Paul was learn to polish gemstones. For many years I had been fascinated by rocks with crystals. There were not many where we lived in Dent County. One time while we lived in St. Louis I picked up a *Lapidary Journal* magazine that was laying in a chair. On the cover was a gemstone carving of a pink rose with a faceted dewdrop and jade leaves. I was so impressed I looked all around to see if it belonged to someone. A young man asked if he could have his magazine back as he was leaving, so I copied down the address of the publisher so I could order the magazine for myself.

Ken bought me a little Rock Rascal for polishing stones and made a sturdy table for it. It would end up in the space where the first kitchen was, and where the little girls' room had been in the little house on St. Paul Street.

We found a store in St. Louis that sold supplies and small slabs to be cut up to make cabochons for jewelry. With the magazine I found rock shows, and from there we found a rock club.

I turned out some really nice cabochons for jewelry so when we were on the way to Salem one time we were going to stop at a little rock shop. It turned out they wanted to go out of business and were ready to sell. We did not have the money but thought some friends of ours might be interested. When we told them, they did not want to go into business but were willing to loan us the money.

A Good While Back

We borrowed $3,000 and rented a small shop space near the Post Office in Columbia.

The little shop, which we named Columbia GRMS (Gems, Rocks and Minerals) seemed sort of out of the way and I never made enough money to keep it going. I did turn out some really pretty cabochons which I mounted in jewelry findings. A few people were interested in the larger rocks that had some really pretty and colorful crystals.

I was taken advantage of a couple of times when someone convinced me to sell some of the special large rock crystal formations at what they called wholesale prices.

When it seemed we were not making enough money to pay the rent we moved the whole thing to our living room at home.

Part II

Chapter 18

After we retired we were having more health issues, especially in respect to achy joints. Ken had ruined his knees mowing that little hill and reconfiguring the back side of the hill into terraces for easier gardening. He was always doing something or building something and it eventually took a toll on his body. I think my hip joints were genetically slightly off kilter and wore out earlier than some would have. Also I did lead a pretty active life. I had said of raising six children, I was tired a lot. Since we could no longer take care of the property on Saint Paul as we felt should be done, we began to look for a way to make some changes in the house especially.

When we checked with the bank we found they would not loan us money to update the house to fit our changing needs. They would, however, loan us money to build a new house. With the help of a realtor we were able to negotiate with a builder to use the old place as down payment, choose a small lot he owned, and have him build a new house for us.

Ken liked to draw things. He had built mostly small cedar boxes and shelves for various things and made detailed plans for each one. He continued to build things through the years and made plans for each project before he started. He had taken a drafting course at the junior college and seemed to me to be pretty good at it. I hoped he would continue with that study.

A Good While Back

He had several books on home building and had actually been working on house plans through the years. He had considered geodesic design, homes partially built underground, and other trends. We had discussed the different problems with the old house, whether real or just personal preference. So he had plans for the new house, considering the small lot and the features we especially wanted right away.

I had worked for the VA for several years and while not actually having anything to do with widening the halls or making other adjustments to the veteran's housing I was aware of the possible need for this sort of thing. So since we were retired and aware of some of the things we might eventually need it was taken into account as we planned the new house.

I am not sure when he did it, but Ken actually drafted the plans for the new house, even knowing where the boards for the major plan were to be placed. While the new house was not completely handicap adapted, certain things were included so major changes would hopefully not be needed later.

Part II

Chapter 19

Because Ken was retired by now he was able be at the new house site every day to watch, photograph, and I'm sure, assess the work being done. Later, when I needed the date the new house had been built I found it in our library along with the many pictures of the house in progress. The house was built in 1994.

Finally the big moving day came. We had known the approximate date for the move but at the last minute we found that the new owners for the house we had sold had to move quickly because they needed to be out of their house on a specific date. It made for a good bit of chaos. Several of our young people and their families came to help. It was hard to pack ahead of time because we actually used most things up to the last minute. Things were packed hastily and put in marked boxes, with the expectation that they could be easily found this way.

The moving truck was loaded and things were moved to Temple Street all in one day. It took nearly all day.

There had been things in the yard I wanted to take to the new place. We had been on "rock hunts" and had found some very interesting rocks I wanted to keep. It turned out someone picked up rocks from the wrong place and the better rocks were left behind.

Some of the new Irises were also left behind but two colors did make it to the Temple Street address.

Some of Ken's special things were left behind, too. He had an old workbench in the newer part of the basement. On it were small pieces of tin from some project or other as well as other odds and ends he thought he might need at a later time. I am sure there were other things he would have preferred to have available in case he would need them.

We get attached to things, and even some inconsequential things take on more importance at times.

After all the activity of moving, the fairly large group was hungry. We cobbled something together and everyone ate.

Boxes were everywhere, and we had no curtains on the windows to provide privacy. We hung a couple of bed sheets to partially cover the windows about the time it was getting dark.

Several in the group stayed and helped put things into a more usable order the next day.

PART II

Chapter 20

Not long after we moved into the new house our Sunday School department decided to have a surprise house warming for us. The fairly large group from Westview Baptist Church came to the house with a gift of a really pretty gold colored table lamp. They also brought a nice bunch of canned goods. The unusual part of that was that they had taken the labels off of all the cans. For many days I would open one can and then decide what to put with it to make a meal. It was actually kind of fun.

It took Ken a little while to get used to our new situation. Again he was into planning and making shelves. He made shelves for the garage, and it was amazing how much stuff he could put away. His carpentry and car repair tools were stored for easy access. There was also room for some of my rock slabbing and polishing tools as well as some of the slabs themselves.

One of the most special sets of shelves he built was for a library. The southwest corner of the new house had double bay windows. The shelves were configured so there was a kind of small private space with plenty of room for a couple of chairs and a small table. The way Ken put up those shelves is still amazing to me. He knew the principal of the lever, so that must be how he did it. I tried to help him put up a smaller, high one. I was so scared. I thought we were losing it but he just kept pushing and we got it up there without having it fall back on us.

A Good While Back

The library was Ken's special place. Early on there were a couple of times when I couldn't find him but knew he was in the house. I would call and he would be back there.

Around the year 2000 Ken started having serious problems with his heart. While he was in the hospital having something checked, one of the students heard a heart murmur. When it was checked thoroughly it turned out to be a leaky heart valve.

It was decided that he needed heart surgery. He went to Christian Hospital Northwest for the procedure. For some reason I felt he would be okay and wasn't too worried during the surgery. When they got inside his chest they decided not to use a pig's valve and instead used a Dacron band around the heart valve to stabilize it. They had cracked the chest and all that would have to knit back together.

The heart valve repair was the start of several procedures that impacted Ken's quality of life. He had prostate cancer and needed several three-times-a-week radiation treatments.

About this time I had an ovarian cyst removed. It was just before Ken was to have three-way heart bypass surgery. My surgeon was sure I would want to be there for him. The kids made sure I got to be with him after his surgery, which was a day or two following my dismissal from the hospital.

Ken had his surgery, with two weeks in the hospital and two weeks of physical and occupational therapy. During this time the kids made sure there was someone to take me to St. Mary's hospital and pick me up so I could be with him every day while he was there.

He had hip replacement surgery. Later he had a procedure where they stopped his heart to try to regulate it so he would no longer have irregular heartbeats. Also during this time he had cataracts removed…and these two procedures did not go very well so he had to have second treatments to both his eyes. These things happened mostly at three or four year intervals so that his health was gradually going down hill.

Ken liked to read and watch the people walking and driving past our house. He also liked to have his coffee in his special chair. He would doze off while holding his cup, and the cup would tip and spill. A couple of times when I found him asleep I tried to take the cup away but he would always awaken and take his cup back.

Ken would get very aggravated because he could not read as he wanted to and would doze off so much of the time. I could tell that he was getting weaker. When we went to church he would take three steps or so and would need to stop to catch his breath.

He got a Rollator walker that could be turned into a transport chair and used it when he went to get the mail. Our mailbox was with others a little way down the street. The Rollator was a little heavy and had to be folded to fit into the car trunk when he wanted to take it somewhere.

We felt we were not getting anywhere with Ken's heart doctor because most of what he seemed to be saying was that Ken needed to lose weight. When that doctor decided to leave the group that we used, we decided not to follow him to his new office because it was not really easy to get to since our driving skills were beginning to be less dependable.

Ken's "new doctor" was two people: One was a regular heart doctor and one was a specialist. To me one problem was that when the doctor was not available a Nurse Practitioner was the one seeing him. These people searched mightily and finally found an irregular heartbeat and wanted to do the heart stopping procedure to try to get his heart beating in a regular manner when it was started again.

Ken was still going steadily down hill even with the new medication they prescribed. His heart rate would be almost normal after walking the long hall to get to the doctor's office. Under regular activity his heart rate would be very slow. He was feeling so bad that we finally went to try to see his heart specialist. The Nurse Practitioner did not seem to recognize anything wrong with his symptoms and wanted him to continue with his new medication.

Sometime that day we needed a few groceries and I offered to go. Ken said, "What, are you trying to take away my job?"

By now he could not lift his Rollator into the trunk of the car

A Good While Back

and would not let me help him. When we got to the office of his regular doctor the next day I was able to talk Ken into letting me get a wheelchair from the lobby for him to use to get inside. He used it like a walker to get to the doctor's office and when he went inside he actually sat in it.

Again the doctor did not see anything unusual with Ken having something almost like blackout spells.

When we got back to the car Ken let me take the wheelchair back to the lobby and he was going to bring the car up to the door. As he was coming near he ran over the little sidewalk curb.

As I got into the car I asked if he wanted me to drive. He said he was sitting down and he was fine. I told him he couldn't drive like that on the highway. He said he knew but he was okay.

I watched Ken's driving as we headed home. He did indeed do fine and we arrived home safely.

The mail had come to our mailbox and I was busy fixing supper. Ken went to get the mail. I had been listening lately to make sure he got to the door safely; again he seemed not to have a problem.

We had supper and were watching TV. Three times he got up and stood by his chair as if he were trying to ward off those spells. After the last one he sat down and gave me a sad, apologetic little smile. I gave him the most bright, encouraging smile I could, not knowing what his look was trying to tell me.

We started to get ready for bed.

Part III
I Will Always Remember

Kenneth (Kenny/Ken)

Kenneth Edwards, c. 1940

Remembering Kenneth

Chapter 1

I have this little voice or notion in my head that says, "Don't forget me." As if I ever could. I spent most of my life with Kenneth Edwards, so I assume the voice or notion in my head is from him. I will spend the rest of my life remembering, probably to the point of getting extremely boring when I speak of him. I have heard other widows doing this and it seems as natural as breathing.

He is gone now and I am left to pick up the pieces, put together a new kind of life for myself and carry on for a while. As I write this it is April, 2013. It was two months ago that Ken collapsed in our bedroom as he was turning down the top cover on the bed.

The paramedics did manage to get a heartbeat but the doctor on duty at the hospital kept saying that he was a very sick man.

Kenneth quit breathing on February 6, 2013. Three of our children were with me at the hospital when he passed.

We had more than 63 years together. We have six grown offspring and their families and many pictures to prove it. I am still trying to do many things as he did—mainly because there are so many things that I had not done before—and needed guidance to get started. In addition to that because we got married young we learned many things together.

I had been working on my own history and in August of 2012 I decided I really needed to try to get something going for Ken. It seemed like a good idea to try to do a taped interview that could be

A Good While Back

added to my story. Then I discovered I had tried to do something like that in 1977, so I started adding to that. It turned out to not be a good idea, though, because there was a roaring sound on the old tape.

At some point I switched to a newer tape but Ken really did not like to talk about himself and at that point his memory had declined in a major way.

Chapter 2

Kenneth Carl Edwards Interview

June 19, 1977

Interviewing Kenneth Edwards regarding some of his younger memories.

O: Would you tell us something about the earliest things that you remember from your childhood?

K: Some of the earliest things I don't think I would want you to know about. I probably don't even remember them.

O: Those things don't count. You're only supposed to tell us things you remember.

K: Well I remember when I was a little kid we had wheat storage bins in the barn and it was a lot of fun for us to jump into those bins. In place of sand we jumped into wheat. 'Course I don't think that was too good, but we did.

O: What do you remember about your brother and sister at that time—back as far as you can remember?

A Good While Back

K: I think that my brother and I—I had an older brother—had to sleep together and we were always fighting about space in the bed or pulling covers or something of the sort. I guess we were always fighting. Probably got along all right though.

O: Did you get along better with your sister?

K: Well, her being a girl I don't know whether you count that as getting along or not. I don't really remember. I guess we got along all right. That's been an awful long time ago.

O: What do you remember of your grandparents…some of the early memories of your grandparents?

K: I guess I really don't remember too much about my grandmother on Mom's side. I kind of remember the day she died. We'd gone to town. It was one of our treats; we got to go to the picture show. And I was in the picture show. I think I had already been through it once and I was sitting through it a second time and my sister came in to get me…to find me to tell me that Grandma died. We, of course, went right out there.

O: Out where?

K: Out to Grandma and Grandpa Grogan's house.

O: How old were you at this time?

K: I'm not sure. I must have been under ten though. I'm pretty sure I wasn't ten years old yet.

O: Had she been sick?

K: No, I don't think she was. I think she had a hemorrhage, a stomach hemorrhage, that she died from. I don't remember that she'd been sick.

O: What do you remember about your Grandpa Grogan?

Remembering Kenneth

K: It's kind of hard to remember about him, too. I know that he lived to be pretty old. As least I thought he was pretty old. He was...I don't remember if he was 92 or 96 when he died.

O: He died in 1948 was it, or '49? Probably '48.

K: Was that just before we were married?

O: Yeah, we had just started going together.

K: I didn't really remember, couldn't place the time.

I remember one of my uncles had a fear of hospitals and resisted taking him to the hospital. They finally took him to the hospital and my uncle had pictures of the tubes and things hanging out of him and so forth and he thought that was torture and he didn't want to take him. They finally took him to the hospital and it took them quite a while to find out what was wrong with him. One of the things that I think they finally just—I suppose, he just starved to death. What I remember....

O: Was he living alone?

K: No. I mean after they got him to the hospital. He couldn't eat. And they couldn't understand what he was saying and it finally turned out he had a growth or something on his tongue that kept him from swallowing. It took a long time to find that and I guess with all the other things, why, it was too late to save him. He died in the hospital.

O: Was he a tough man or a gentle man? You must have known him before.

K: I don't personally remember, but I remember some of the things Mom said about him. I think he was pretty tough. As far as just what you call toughness. Course I don't remember personally.

A Good While Back

O: How about the Edwards grandparents?

K: I was around them more, I suppose than I was around the other side of the family and knew them after I was older. So I would have later memories of them.

O: Are there any characteristics you remember about your Grandpa Edwards? One or two, like his ideas?

K: Oh, I think he was a pretty strong Republican. It didn't make too much difference if there was a Democrat in office. Well, you could bet that Grandpa didn't approve of the way he was running things, no matter what office. Grandma was always little.

O: Maybe she shrunk in her later years. She was always—

K: Well, I always remember her as little. Maybe she did shrink but she wasn't too big to start with. She always seemed to be, I always remember her as being kind of weak. Seemed fragile to me.

O: Sickly?

K: Well, not sickly. Just fragile I guess you would say. But she lived to a pretty good old age. Quite a bit longer than the doctors expected.

O: What was her attitude toward your grandpa?

K: Well I just don't know what you would say her attitude was. She was a...

O: My impression was protective.

K: I can't say that I—

O: Even though he was the stronger.

K: Well he was the man in the family, I suppose, and seemingly they played out the roles of man and woman like you used to think of them rather than now where the woman is supposed to be liberated and so forth. I don't suppose they thought anything about that. She was the woman, took care of the house and the man took care of the heavy work.

O: What about your own childhood, now. Can we go back to that? Can you remember anything, generally how things went at home? Were your parents strict? Did you have work to do?

K: Well I suppose I thought I had more work than was necessary, but really, I suppose that I was more protected, didn't have too much to do, really.

O: What were some of the things that you did do, like jobs or —

K: Well, I suppose feeding the chickens was one of my jobs and a few things like that. If I remember right my sister and I had to wash dishes before we went to school. And just things like that. We had to haul the water for the tomato plants and the sweet potato plants when we were growing them, at least part of the time.

O: Did you help plant the garden in the spring?

K: Well, I, yes I guess I was in on it, but I didn't do as much of it as I should have, I suppose. I probably thought I was having to do too much, it was too hot, and so on and so forth.

O: Do you remember specifically though. Did you think these things?

K: I'm sure I did.

O: How was school? Can you describe your schoolhouse?

K: I usually got along pretty good in school and liked most of my teachers most of the time and was always interested in schoolwork, I guess. I always wanted to read.

O: What kind of school did you go to, grade school?

K: Well, it was a country school. And it had all the eight grades in one school, and one teacher. And we had different times, took turns reciting and so forth. We had study times while other classes were having their time to recite. I believe most of the time in grade school I didn't have very many in my class. 'Course in our community there wasn't too many people moving in and out. It never changed too much. It started out in a class about the same bunch of kids stayed in the class all the way through. There'd be some move, some move out. I was by myself for a good deal of the seven years.

O: How did the teacher handle this unusual class?

K: Well, it didn't take too long to recite. Didn't have to take too many turns for that.

O: You had a regular class period, though, like all the others?

K: It was just there wasn't as many of us. I guess part of the time I had Kenneth Brummett in my class. It does seem like there was a girl in there for one year but I don't remember who.

O: Where was Ellen Brooks?

K: I suppose that Ellen Brooks would have graduated with that class but only the last year I was counted in that class. Technically I took two years in one year, two class years in one year. The first half of the year I was in one class and the last half they moved me up to the class that should have been a year ahead of me.

O: Did you have to do extra work or was it just that you could handle the work that they were doing?

K: I think it was just that I could handle what it was. I think for me to graduate from the eighth grade, to get approval, they had to go clear to the state level—the state superintendent—to get permission for me to graduate a year ahead.

O: What do you remember about recess and the school grounds and any interesting experiences and/or games you played with the other kids?

K: Well, we always had recess—morning and afternoon of course—and during the season we'd play ball, at least part of them would play ball. I'm not sure what all games we'd play. Marbles, we played marbles.

O: That wasn't a special game somehow?

K: Well I remember some of it, not too much. I guess I wasn't too good a marble player.

O: Was this exclusively a boy's game?

K: I don't know exclusively or not. It does seem like it was the boys that played marbles. 'Don't remember if the girls had their game or not. I don't think we played together. That wouldn't have been…'course I don't remember if they did or not. Maybe they did. Probably. I remember that I borrowed a special marble from you one time and got it broke.

O: Are you sure that wasn't one of the little cute gifts I passed on to you through your sister?

K: No, I'm pretty sure that was one that I just borrowed from you to use for recess or something and somebody hit it real hard and broke it.

O: What about other games and other people? Do you remember anything in particular that was interesting? Incidents and….

A Good While Back

K: No. There was one time. Jimmy Norris had brought his football to school and we got to play with it, and then I think some of the bigger boys started using a ball bat on it. They hit it with a ball bat. I don't remember if it was James Hofer or Gene Land that finally busted it with the bat. And they put it under one of the bases on the ball field and tried to hide it. I don't think I told who tried to hide it. The big boys, of course, didn't admit they had broke his football.

O: What do you remember of the lunchroom facilities?

K: I don't know that we really had lunchroom facilities. Most of the kids brought their own lunch. I guess the ones that had lunch had to bring them. I guess in the wintertime we had to eat at our desks or had to go to somebody else's desk. In the summer time we just scattered out and ate lunch wherever you could.

O: Do you remember anything about the lunches that was unusual, yours or anyone else's?

K: No, I never did pay that much attention to the lunches, I don't think.

O: How about the restroom facilities.

K: Well, it was about like what we had at home. It was a house down at the end of the path. The boys' was down in one corner and the girls' was down in another corner. Pretty well separated. 'Couldn't see them from each other I don't think.

O: What do you remember about the drinking facilities, the water supply?

K: We had a bucket of water. I remember the old well. Some of the older boys would have to go draw out the water, if I'm not mistaken. I'm trying to remember. Maybe we had our own water cups. Had to pour the water in our cups from the dipper.

O: At one time was there a crockery fountain with a push button, or not?

K: That I don't remember.

O: Do you remember the old well house?

K: I kind of remember the old well house, yes.

O: Do you remember why it had to be removed and what was used to replace it?

K: No, I can't say that I do. You were there several years after I was.

O: Do you remember the peach tree at the corner of the schoolhouse?

K: Yeah, I think I remember the peach tree. It was an Indian Peach tree I think.

O: Do you remember the old organ in the schoolroom?

K: Yeah, I do kind of remember it now that you mention it, but I don't remember anybody playing it. I remember the little shelves on it, I think.

O: Do you remember what the heating stove was like?

K: I know we had a wood stove in the middle of the room. I really don't remember the shape of it. I don't remember if it had the old traditional shape, I don't think it was the old potbelly stove, though.

O: Do you remember it as being oval and sort of tall with a steel jacket around it?

K: I'm not sure about that either.

O: Do you remember the library?

A Good While Back

K: The only library that I remember was a few shelves with a few books on it. I don't remember too much about a library. That might have been, but that is the impression that I remember—just four or five shelves, and not very long shelves.

O: Do you remember the Christmas programs and end of school plays? Did you participate in these?

K: Oh, yes, if I remember right I never was an actor. I was too self-conscious to be an actor but I was in most of them, one way or the other.

O: What was the curtain for these productions?

K: I believe, originally, when I was in the earlier grades, they just had a curtain on a wire that some of the bigger ones would take hold of and move back. But I believe that before I left they had put in a curtain and pulled it with a rope, like you open the drapes, Something like that.

O: That wasn't a roll up curtain that had ropes and pulley or something like that?

K: I think I might have confused the schools, one school with another school. I believe you might be right about the roll up deal where it was a rope around the end of a tube or a metal drain pipe or something that rolled up with a curtain. It wasn't a cloth curtain, was it? It was something more like an oilcloth, wasn't it.

O: Yes, or more like cloth covered with plastic, sort of like oilcloth but not quite as slick, maybe.

K: Yeah. Something like that.

O: Were there cabinets with doors in the front of the room behind the teacher's desk?

K: Yes.

O: What were these used for?

K: That I don't remember. I remember that at one time they had a special play. I think some of the adults in the community had worked up a play. I don't remember if it was for a pie supper. I don't remember what it was. But I think that this was on the night they had their performance: They had their kerosene mantle light setting on top of the cabinet. It was supposed to have metal—a piece of metal—on the ceiling over it where the heat of the chimney went up and hit the metal. Somebody had got the light scooted over a little bit and it caught the ceiling on fire. It was smoking. Everett [Ken's brother] noticed it during the play. He reached up to one of the men on the stage, sitting on the couch I believe, and at first the man didn't understand. They finally got through to him there was a fire up there—finally got him to looking—and before it actually broke into a fire, they got it stopped.

O: This was with a crowd in the building?

K: Oh, yes, there would have been. I don't remember if it was a great big crowd but it would have been several people. The whole community would have been there, most of them.

O: Was everything done in this one room, like for these pie suppers you mentioned and the plays?

K: Well originally it was, but I don't know what grade I was in. They had a two year high school there. That building was big enough that they actually had two rooms in the building. One was the grade school and the other was the high school. Sometime while I was going to school they cut an opening between the two rooms—opened up between the two of them—and had removable doors. They would take the partition out and open up both rooms for any pie suppers and so forth. That made a lot more room.

O: Could you describe one of the pie suppers—the purpose and generally what went on?

K: Well, they'd have pie suppers to raise money and the different girls and women would bake a pie. Most of them were pies. They had a few cakes. They'd be in a fancy box all wrapped up real nice and, theoretically, nobody knew which girl had brought which pie. And they would have an auctioneer, someone to sell the pies. They'd have a play or entertainment of some sort and then have their pie auction. And they'd hold the pie up—some of them were kind of plain boxes and others were fancied up to look pretty—and they'd auction them off. Sometimes the man, or boy, would know whose pie they were bidding on because it was their girlfriend's pie, and if someone else found out that this was their girlfriend's, why they ran the price up. Sometimes they would have to dig deep or even borrow money to buy it. They had to; it was embarrassing for someone else to get your girlfriend's pie.

Chapter 3

Continuation of interview with Kenneth Edwards
August 29, 2012

O: Who were your playmates when you lived back on the farm?

K: Well that, having to try to remember, we had pretty much the family; we saw people at church; we saw Forest and their family; Uncle Archie. I don't recall his wife's name…

O: It was Anna.

K: Anna

O: Yes, his first wife was Anna.

K: Who were the kids? Irene and…

O: Lonnie

K: Yeah, Lonnie.

O: Named after your grandpa?

K: Yeah it must have been, I guess later on he actually spent time in the service. He died from an operation, I think it was. I don't remember what the operation was for, but he didn't wake up from the operation. I just don't remember what the operation was for. I knew at the time. I don't remember how old I was at the time. He was much older than me.

O: It was a burst appendix, wasn't it?

K: I just don't remember what he was supposed to have had.

O: Did he play with you guys much or was it just the kids your age?

K: The kids my age. Jim, Jimmy, was down the other direction, I guess you'd say. Pretty much Saturday afternoon we would go to town and Jim's family would be in town. Saturday afternoon a lot of times I would go home with Jim and spend the night and then go to church on Sunday. Sunday we would go to church at Doss.

O: Were there other relatives that lived nearby?

K: Yeah, I'm sure Aunt Lennie and her family lived down nineteen [State Highway 19] and let's see they must have lived past... down to Gladden. That's funny I don't remember, I'm pretty sure it was on 19, though. There was Hertha and Dallas.

O: Was Dallas close to your age?

K: No, he would have been several years older than me.

O: What kind of car did you drive? Did your dad drive? Did your family have?

K: Sometime in there Dad had a Model T, I guess it was. I guess we went to....

O: Did you all go to town in the Model T? It sounds like you would have been hanging off the sides or something. There were five of you. Did your mom go to town with you?

K: I'm sure she did. I remember we had two ways to get to town.

Remembering Kenneth

O: Out past your Uncle Archie's.

K: Yeah, that was one way, and seems like when it was bad weather we could come down to Highway 19, turn onto B Highway and come in on B; but I think that would have been quite a bit further and I think most of the time we'd come in the other way. B Highway hadn't been upgraded yet. It was still a country road. Boy, not being able to remember this stuff is kind of...I wasn't paying enough attention when I was growing up, I guess.

O: What did you pay attention to? What was your interest growing up? What were your interests?

K: Well, I don't remember. What did I do? Oh, I guess somewhere in there Uncle Homer and his family must have lived up in the Pasley house. Sometime or other I must have played with Peggy. She must have been close to my age, maybe. Bill would have been a couple of years older.

O: What kind of games did you play when they came to visit? Did they come on Sunday? Did you have family gatherings and play marbles, tag, what did you do?

K: Well, I'm kind of drawing a blank. I don't know what kind of games we played.

O: When did you move to town?

K: I guess we moved to town when I was ready to go into high school. [We] moved to town so I could go to high school.

O: We had high school at Warfel.

K: I didn't go to Warfel.

O: Maybe it was so Naomia could go too. Was she two years ahead of you or just one?

A Good While Back

K: Now I guess that could have been. I don't remember that well. Boy, I had a lost childhood, I guess.

O: You're the only one to remember it now. What did you do in town? You didn't have the woods to walk in, the chickens to feed, or did you?

K: For a while, sometime there, we had a young cow we kept on a neighbors lot. I remember milking a cow.

O: Did you share the milk with the neighbor for using their lot?

K: I don't know what the arrangements would have been.

O: How was school? Did you have sports?

K: Well, we had sports. I wasn't good enough for the basketball team. Then the softball team....

O: Was that the school team or the county team?

K: That was the county team. And we had a baseball team for the high school, too, I think. And we also had an American Legion team. I played for another team. I rode the bus over to Potosi, to play on the American Legion team.

O: The school bus?

K: Well, no we had a bus service down there. I don't know how far it went. We'd catch the bus there in Salem, ride it over to Steelville, and catch another bus going to Potosi. I guess that must have been on a Sunday. Ball games on Sunday. I'd forgotten about that.

O: Do you remember some of the people on the team, the names?

K: Oh, I guess the one who was close to being notable was, [chuckles] I can't think of his name. I think he did play some for a professional team. He was good enough to.

O: Was that Roby Vaughan?

K: No, Roby Vaughan was on our Salem team in the county league. No, Roby was on the Doss team. Doss had a team.

O: Which team were you on then? How many teams were you on?

K: That's pretty good. I was playing on the town team, I think, and all my relatives were on the Doss team. They had a pretty good team for Doss.

O: Would that have been one of the county teams, too, playing against Salem?

K: I guess Salem was in a bigger league. We had county teams like Doss, Deep Ford, Turtle and what were their [the other teams'] names? We had six or eight teams. Salem was in a league that had teams like Salem, Licking, you know, the bigger teams.

O: Steelville?

K: I guess. I don't particularly remember that we played in Steelville. Licking was one that we played, too. Anyway, they were a step up from the county team.

O: Which did you play with?

K: Well, I started with the town, then I switched from them. I quit the town team and joined the Doss team. I guess at the time it was a mistake. I should have stayed with the town team.

O: But the family members were with the Doss team? Right?

K: Yeah, yeah, Bill Raulston. Doc Raulston was his dad.

O: Jim probably came in there somewhere.

K: Yeah, and that would have been the one where we had Roby Vaughn and Everett Hasting.

O: They were on the Doss team?

K: Lets see, Darien was one of our arch rivals, I guess you'd say.

O: One of the store and school communities.

K: Darien was a store, and sometime in there they had a skating rink.

Chapter 4

O: What else were activities when you lived in town? Swimming, and watching the girls, and taking pictures?

K: Well, yeah. I had a year or two that I spent a lot of time at the swimming pool.

O: Swimming or just taking pictures of the girls?

K: I guess I swam most of the time. A year or two I had the camera. I guess I was fifteen, somewhere around there.

O: When did you and Stanford Sheets set up your own darkroom?

K: Oh, He had that enlarger. He helped me set up the darkroom.

O: Where was the darkroom?

K: It was in the little bathroom or the half-bath on the second floor.

O: In the house on Pershing?

K: Yeah, I think it was.

O: Was he born with the knowledge? Where did you learn how to make pictures? Whatever you do, process the film, make the pictures? You did all that in that little tiny bathroom?

A Good While Back

K: Yeah, it wasn't very big, but, that was my education, I guess. Stan knew a little bit about it and I guess I would have been reading at the time.

O: On stuff from the library, magazines. Where did you find the information?

K: Magazines, I guess, was one of the main things. Boy, a lot of that is kind of murky. I just don't remember all that.

O: Sounds like you are remembering enough of it, though, for it to be interesting.

K: Yeah. I still have the camera I got.

O: And that developed into a lifelong interest, right?

K: Yeah, an interest but not enough to be serious about it. It was just enough to be interested in it. Just like my flying, wanting to fly. Wanting to read about it and not enough to actually do it.

O: Were there other hindrances to the furthering of your interest?

K: More the wanting to read about it than to actually do it.

O: I thought maybe it was access and money.

K: Well, it would have been money, yeah, but there are a lot of others you read about that cared enough about it to work and do what it took to do it. I was too lazy to do that, I guess, or afraid to do it.

Chapter 5

O: So what do you remember about fixing up the upstairs on the Pershing Avenue house for our first apartment for when we were getting married.

K: I really don't remember that much about it. I guess Dad did most of the work.

O: I thought it was you and your mom. It would have had to be your dad, I guess. He would have had to drive the nails. Was there water in the kitchen part of that? Or did we have to get the water? Did we have a refrigerator? I guess I don't remember that much about it either.

K: I guess I don't remember anything. Did we have a refrigerator?

O: Stove? I remember cabinets in there, probably a table. I don't remember the other stuff though, the sink, the stove, the refrigerator....

K: Yeah, what would we have had for the stove? I just don't remember that. Boy!

O: Do you remember the adventure of our moving to St. Louis? How that situation worked out? Do you remember the apartment or the bus? The neighbors.

A Good While Back

K: Yeah. We rode the bus down with our stuff in a suitcase. Naomia and Aunt Lennie met us at the bus station and took us on the city bus to where their rooming house was. And for six months or so we took the bus. And bummed a ride from somebody else, riding back to Salem. Oh, my, there's….

O: Oh, yes, I'd forgotten about that. Do you remember, didn't we ride with Wilber one time in an old convertible? It was breezy and rainy. And did he have a flat tire and was stopping anyway or did we slide off the road?

K: I don't think we slid off the road, but we did ride with him that weekend. It was, I don't really remember that situation; I do remember he had that convertible.

O: I remember it was a leaky convertible, at least in the rain.

K: It actually leaked? I don't remember.

O: Who else did we ride with?

K: I guess we rode with somebody that Jackie knew for one thing. There have been a lot of things—looking back on things—I wish I could do a do over and do different.

O: After your folks did their sharecropping or whatever then you moved to town and built a nice new house. What was that about? How did they do that?

K: (Laugh) I suppose when we moved to town we rented a couple of places. 'Guess we rented a couple of places, then moved back to the farm, then built the house. Huh, have to think on that a while.

O: And they used oak like my folks did.

K: Well, I think we cut our own lumber.

O: Trees for lumber?

K: Yeah.

O: That would have come off the eighty acres that they gave us, then wouldn't it?

K: Yeah, I guess so. I don't remember that part really. That whole thing is more or less speculation, I guess, how it was and how it got there. I don't know.

O: Parents didn't discuss those things with the kids. In Don's tape he seemed to know about some of those things. I didn't.

K: He probably paid more attention.

O: He helped, apparently. You didn't have to pull or hold up the other end of the saw, I guess. Did you still have a cow when you moved to the new house?

K: Well that might have been when we got the cow or brought the cow in from the farm. That is probably how we got the cow in town, used one that we had on the farm. Dad more or less stayed on the farm or he spent most of his time out on the farm.

O: Almost like commuting.

K: Yeah, only he knew that it was far out. What would it have been? Ten miles. He didn't try to drive back and forth every day. He would go out and stay for a week. He didn't have a job in town, I guess, so his job was farming.

O: A little later he tried to have a taxi cab service.

K: Yeah, that was one of the jobs Dad did. He worked for Uncle Homer in the grocery store. And when Homer put in the slaughterhouse, he was the one that did that. That's the job I would come after school and help with, the work at the slaughterhouse during high school.

O: Did you help with the preparation of all of them? What was your part?

K: All the way from getting them out of the pen and bringing them into the slaughterhouse and shooting them and slitting their throats, scalding them and scraping off the hide.

O: If they were already dead why did you have to slit their throats?

K: To get the blood out. [softly] You knew that.

O: [laughing] Well, I thought it might need to come out in the story, though. Not everyone would know. But you knew how to cut up the various steaks, hams and shoulders.

K: Well, the slaughterhouse that's mostly just dressed up: taking out the entrails (all the insides) and hanging. 'Didn't cut them up. Actually started up at the end of the war. Uncle Homer got the permit to start a slaughterhouse to be able to butcher. He would cut them up; he was the butcher in the store.

O: That's why he needed the slaughterhouse because he had his own store.

K: Yeah. He figured it would be more economical to do his own butchering than to buy it from a wholesaler.

O: What all kinds of butchering did you do, mostly pigs?

K: Pigs, cows, calves. Mostly pigs. I don't remember doing lambs. All I remember learning how to do was pigs. Pigs and shoats.

O: Did they use any of the entrails? I think the Germans cleaned out the intestines for casings for sausage.

K: I don't think so. I guess if someone wanted them saved it would have been an easy enough thing if someone wanted to work them up. Like the liver and stuff?

O: You always saved those didn't you? The brains? Saved the whole head?

K: Yeah.

O: And what did you do with the hooves and the entrails and—

K: Thinking back on it now I don't remember what all we got rid of. I suppose we got rid of it somehow. Huh. I don't remember what we did.

O: Did you also work at Homer's store part-time?

K: Yeah. I don't remember what year. He had some of the nephews be helpers at the store. I had a couple of years of being the one that had the job.

O: Stock boy?

K: Well, stock boy, doing things, selling stuff, filling orders.

O: What's the difference in selling stuff and filling orders? That's waiting on customers.

K: Well, people would drop off their lists and I would get stuff off the shelves and write it up and…

O: It wasn't like in today's supermarkets where you go to get your own?

K: Yeah, like most of it wasn't like where you read off your list and get your own stuff. Course now it would be inefficient.

O: Did you always have a cash register or did you do your own figuring?

A Good While Back

K: Well that was before they started the automatic cash register stuff.

O: They had little adding machines and things to help. I know the Alexanders had a cash register. Now whether they just put the total in I'm not sure or whether it was part adding machine.

K: I don't think they were used for an adding machine.

O: So just putting the total in or something?

K: For making change or something. Well, you did your own figuring. Wrote it down and added it up, wrote it up.

O: Did you have friends in high school? Still go to the picture show on Saturday, and….

K: Well, I don't know. I guess I would still get to see the switch when they had a new movie on. Try to go. That's when I was getting in for a dime.

O: That's going back a ways. Did you still have family gatherings, go to see your grandparents on weekends, Sundays or whatever?

K: Uhhh, let's see…I'm trying to remember about that—

[end of tape]

Chapter 6

Although I did not know it at the time, Kenneth Carl Edwards was starting life in Dent County at about the same time as me. In fact, he was not many miles from where I lived. He was born in September of 1930, the youngest of three children.

As you can tell, when I interviewed Kenneth he did not remember much about when he was a child. Some pictures in our collection show the three children in his family with what are probably used tires of different sizes. The children appear to have been using them to see how far they could roll them in the dusty area where they were playing.

The first home he said he remembered was a rented farm with a house that was called The Pasley Place. It was sort of on the high end of a ridge and near what we would later know as Doss Store. Later they moved to a larger and possibly more fertile place a couple of miles away. It was also closer to the school.

Both of these farms were on a county road, and Kenneth remembered something of the building of this road. It was between the house and the barn. Apparently it was originally a dirt road which was later upgraded to gravel. Since travel on that road was very light for a long time, most of the time it was probably a place to play.

There were, of course, visits from relatives in the area. His mother and his father came from very large families themselves and in most of the younger families there were at least two children.

A Good While Back

Kenneth's mother, Daphnia Irene Grogan, was from a family with thirteen children. Kenneth's dad, Carl Alonzo Edwards, was from a family of nine or ten children. One of Kenneth's best friends through most of his life was Jimmy Edwards, a double cousin of a number difficult to count.

When he was young, Kenny and Jimmy liked to play cowboys and Indians. We even still have Kenny's original cap gun. At one time they decided to build a log cabin. They were a little older by then but their "logs" were probably only three or four inches in diameter. In the photo we have, their log cabin looks a little drafty.

Another thing Kenny did was go to the cowboy movies in town with his friends on Saturday afternoons. Kenny's family would go to Salem, probably to spend the day. That allowed him to attend movies starring Roy Rogers and Gene Autry.

Kenny was two years ahead of me in high school, so while I was in school at the country high school he was finishing his last two years in Salem High School. I was not keeping up with what was going on in his life but normal things were going on with him too.

He was already interested in cameras and girls. Kenneth took pictures at the swimming pool. His Uncle Stanford Sheets helped him set up a dark room in the tiny bathroom under the eves upstairs of Kenneth's parents' home on Pershing Avenue in Salem. (This would later be a part of our first apartment.) They developed, washed and dried the film, then used a very small enlarger to put the image on photo paper. Then that had to be developed, washed and dried to make the actual photo.

The very small enlarger stayed with us even after basic photo work gave way to color and digital photographs and many other advances. This left me with a lot of obsolete equipment after Ken was gone.

Chapter 7

In some ways it seemed that our last year together might have been our best. We were so in tune with each other and being thoughtful of each other. We were both low on strength and energy and we both did what we could to make things easier for the other.

One night I commented on the fact that my engagement ring was still pretty. (This was after our sixty-third wedding anniversary.) Ken had a smile of appreciation that I still enjoyed the ring.

I felt I had not been pro-active enough when Mom told me her doctor had cut out her blood pressure medicine. Later I would wish I had called to try to find out why he had done that. Because of that, and thinking we were more knowledgeable about medical things, we tried to be careful to ask more questions when Ken was sick. He had been having trouble with his heart for about twelve years.

The doctor's group made some changes and we decided not to follow that doctor to his new location. It turned out that his new doctor was actually two doctors: a regular heart doctor and a specialist. Ken had atrial fibrillation. They had to try really hard to find it. They had him on a new medicine to protect against blood clots. They also had put him through the procedure of stopping the heart and starting it again. He was so weak toward the end of his life that he sometimes would take a few steps and would have to stop to get his breath. He was having enough trouble that we asked for an appointment for him to see his doctor. He was only able to see the nurse practitioner the day before he collapsed.

She insisted he was to continue the medications as he had been doing. The day he collapsed he saw his regular doctor and neither of them recognized the significance of his having spells when he would almost pass out.

On Ken's last night he stood by his chair three times, probably trying to overcome the darkness that was trying to overtake him. Then later he gave me a sad little smile of apology. I think Ken may have known he would not last through the night. I was not so good about catching little signs and gave him the brightest, most reassuring smile I could. I think he appreciated it.

We started to get ready for bed February 5, 2013.

Chapter 8

Ken had a lifelong interest in photography and cameras. A couple of years after we moved to Columbia in November of 1958 he finally had space to put in a full size photo lab. We built an addition to our small house, which made extra space in the old part of the basement. Ken turned that into his darkroom. It was outfitted well and after a while he started his photography business. This was all before color pictures.

He put a roll of background paper on one side of the living room and sometimes people came to the house to have their pictures made. Sometimes he would take wedding pictures. He usually went to churches for those. Those pictures were very good. Meanwhile I got a book and supplies and learned retouching and photo oil coloring.

I do not remember how long he tried to continue the business but it apparently was not earning what it should have to keep it going, so he eventually quit as a business.

He did, however, put in a special darkroom in the new house, which we had built in 1994. He used it some in the new house until his hands started having a reaction to the chemicals. I think his energy level was getting lower by then, too. He had the new darkroom outfitted so he could make really large photos. One of our favorites hangs in the hallway now. It was of the family with Penni in her early teens. She called herself was a giant during that time period. She got her growth a little early.

A Good While Back

We especially like to compare it to later pictures and see how much people have changed or not changed. I did not realize until some of these comparisons how much people are still the same. People are what they are from a very early age.

One of the things Ken kept in the darkroom when we moved to Temple Street was the small enlarger he originally had with his Uncle Stanford in the little darkroom under the eves on Pershing Street.

Ken also studied old time photographers who had made breakthroughs in techniques and understanding lights and darks, shadows and basic photography. He had a major collection of their books. These early pioneers of photography were an inspiration to him and he was able to try some of their ideas. He usually carried a camera with him when he went somewhere.

For a long time Ken would take pictures of family events, but he was rarely included in the pictures himself because he was holding the camera. At times he seemed more interested in nature photos.

For many years he wanted a Leica camera, but he never felt we could afford it. At one point when digital photography had finally gained such a foothold, I asked for one of those cameras. Ken did not want a cheap one. He kept talking about the Leica so I finally told him to go ahead and get one. He did get his Leica but it turned out that it was too advanced electronically for him to understand all the features. He did, however, get some really beautiful pictures. His photos of sunsets, storm clouds, and blue skies with fluffy white clouds are especially interesting.

This turned out to be his last year.

Chapter 9

Ken had an interest in so many things. He loved to read. He read at work when he had the chance. After we moved to Columbia, Ken still worked at Brown Shoe Company in St. Louis, which involved about a twenty-mile one-way trip to go to work. Lunch break was one of the special times when he got to read.

Ken especially liked *National Geographic* magazine and collected them for forty-three years. He finally gave them up when he could no longer keep up with reading them. He still collected other magazines and books.

Ken was interested in airplanes and flying and his magazine and book collection included how-to books on building and flying airplanes. He belonged to the association of amateur builders of airplanes and we went to at least two of their fly-ins. There was a large collection of different kinds of homebuilts, gyrocopters, vintage aircraft, and sometimes factory built larger planes. It was tiring for me but he seemed not to get tired.

One of his early experiences with flying was when he tried to use his Christian witness to win the husband of a lady who was attending the First Baptist Church in Columbia. This fellow had a plane and would ask Ken to fly with him. Ken really did not feel safe flying with the guy and finally had to distance himself from the situation. He felt bad about having to do that but felt he had to protect himself. Several years later he ran into the family. The man had passed away and his wife blamed Ken for the fact that her husband had never become a Christian.

Chapter 10

Ken did several things after we moved to Temple Street. He put in several new fruit trees: a grafted apple tree with four varieties, a peach tree, a tart red cherry tree, and another apple tree with three or four grafts that each produced a different kind of apple. They were small trees because the space at the side of the house was limited.

We enjoyed the fruit from these trees for several years until the trees started dying one by one. The cherry tree and an apple tree with four varieties grafted to the base were the longest lasting. Before the apple tree finally got blight and had to be taken down, two varieties of apples died and those limbs were removed. Of the last two varieties, one made very good apple pies and special tart dried apples. I really missed that tree when it had to be taken out.

Ken continued gardening after the move. Mostly he tried raised bed gardening. It was never very successful because there were several large trees nearby. Also there were other things to hinder it, such as bugs that liked certain plants, squirrels, rabbits and a neighbor's cat that liked to do it's business among our young carrots. The last especially did not set well with me but as the owner of the cat told me: "There are no leash laws in Columbia for cats."

We still had some good things at times and we were slowing down anyway.

Ken built and installed book shelves. We were both readers and enjoyed having space to put the books through the years. The way he put them in at the southern front corner of the house where the two sets of bay windows were, made a kind of nook. He had the floor especially reinforced to hold the weight of filled shelves.

Those shelves housed much fiction, resource books, history books, how-to books on various subjects, and others. We belonged to a Christian book club for a while and that helped us find books we could really enjoy. We also kept special magazines. We did finally have to slow down buying books because we were running out of space.

After Ken passed some of the shelves were popping and cracking so loudly that I began to move the larger books and photo albums to lower shelves and began to give our "kids" some of them. There was also an old youth set of *Encyclopedia Britannica*. I let everyone take the one from their birth year if it was there.

Ken tried to keep up with mowing the lawn but he kept getting slower and slower at that job. By then he had developed heart problems and I started asking Kenny, one of our grandsons, to mow the yard for us. Kenny did not especially like that job but he kept at it until he went away to college.

Ken liked to sit in the library and watch the street and the neighborhood from that space. He could read, or draw or check on the next project.

Ken had built things from a young age. In shop class he had made a cute little set of corner shelves that he gave to his Mom. She went to live with her daughter after a stroke and when Ken's dad was having his auction we got the little shelves.

Drawing those detailed working designs and making things was one of Ken's special interests. He left several drawings of this nature, but without necessarily including any notation of what it was to be when finished.

Chapter 11

Besides being a box maker at Ely Walker in Salem, Ken worked for Brown Shoe Company for thirty years in St. Louis. He was fifty years old and really wanted to retire when the company moved that part of their operation to Arkansas where they could pay their workers less. I'm sure this also had something to do with having to pay union wages.

After a while a friend at church, who was some kind of supervisor at Cerro Copper in Sauget, offered him a job there. Ken worked as a shipping clerk for that company thirteen years. That job involved knowing the weight of certain products in order to not overload a big truck. It sounded pretty involved, because there could be several different types of tubes and pipes on any given load.

Meanwhile, Ken would be trying to do other small business things at home as well as taking care of the garden and yard, and building little things.

In the meantime I was trying to do the mother/housewife things. When these slowed down I tried a couple of things in town. One of these was as a school crossing guard. That was a cold and hard job. After a while my back would hurt from all the standing. I only lasted three years. Next, I tried working for a couple of lawyers in town. I didn't do very well there and got fired.

I think it was then that we tried having the rock shop. That did not last long either, partly because I really did not know how to run a business.

I started taking college classes at night at the high school. Ken joined me in this but dropped out after the first semester. I took several of these and also a class for Certified Nursing Assistant. After I took the classes I thought I needed from the offerings in Columbia, I took a few at the Belleville campus of what was then called Belleville Area College.

This was kind of fun. I was in my forties competing with recent high school graduates and was doing very well.

I did learn an extra couple of things while going to school there. One was the smell of marijuana. One day in science class there was an odd smell in the classroom. Some of the students had the window open a little and were frantically trying to fan the smoke through the open window before the teacher arrived.

Another thing I learned was do not make even a joking threat against the President of the United States when there are some young airmen in the vicinity. One woman did this and found strange things happening. Her old car was broken into and probably searched. Then she was called aside and into a private room and questioned. It was pretty scary for her.

I also took the Civil Service Test with an eye toward possibly getting a government job. I didn't do as well as I thought I could have since I had a cold at the time. I took the test a second time and only did a little better.

In 1982 I got a job as a CNA at the Memorial Convalescent Center in Belleville. Patient care was a very hard job, even part time, even for three months. There was one major snowstorm when the highways were plowed but the side streets were not. So only the out-of-town CNAs made it to work that day. The people were so nice I sort of hated to leave when I was offered a job at Jefferson Barracks Hospital.

The interview at JB was interesting. The regular head of MAS (Medical Administration Service) was on vacation or something, so a substitute interviewed us. This was for a position as transcriptionist doing discharge summaries that had been dictated by the doctors. I had reached the status of number one on the list. I was fifty years old at the time. Thirty-year-old Sherri, who was number two, was also there to be interviewed. I was pretty sure they wanted to hire Sherri for I felt that her skills were probably more current than mine. The special part was that they hired both of us.

I have a lot of memories of those times but for now I'll just say I ended up trying various jobs there, among which were release of information and later in prosthetic service.

I guess prosthetics was my favorite. I have many memories of the various things that were done in that section. I did not have a part in all of them but still learned a lot from the different processes going on around me.

Actually I was a clerk in that section, and for a while most of my job was answering the phone, greeting the veterans who came to the door, and typing up orders for the different products that they needed. I was the wheelchair lady for a while; I think I did very well in that position.

At some point the new assistant chief decided to take over with major measuring and fitting of the wheelchairs. The problem was that at least one turned out to be heavier than the veteran was used to and he couldn't use it. Sometimes more simple is better.

During this time I decided to join an exercise class they offered. It was to be held in an indoor pool that was also used by the veterans who were patients there. The water was as warm as bath water and the room was very humid. One of the several exercises was turning a bent knee toward the other leg. I did that a few times and it hurt my hips so much I could barely walk. After I found a surgeon I decided to have hip replacement surgery and I learned I had enough sick time and vacation time saved so that I only had to take two weeks without pay. My boss had told me to not come back 'till I had both hips done.

When I went back after about three and a half months things just did not seem to click any more. There was just something missing. Ken had already retired at sixty-two years old, and maybe it was partly that which made it harder for me to adjust to being back at work. I had also turned sixty-two and ended up retiring that year a few months before the full twelve years working for the VA.

I have a lot of fond memories of working at the Veterans Administration Medical Center. Besides learning bits and pieces of extra information that were not directly associated with my actual jobs but that turned out to be helpful later, I gained a lot of confidence I didn't have before.

Chapter 12

In addition to the visits to several of the Missouri state parks and their campgrounds we also did a little other traveling. By now Mom and Dad lived in Belvedere, Illinois. We visited them there a few times. Some of the kids had moved to other states and we visited most of them at some time or another.

At one point during her medical training, Penni had a six week course in Silver Spring, Maryland. They invited us up for a week and while Penni was studying, her husband, John, and little Jason showed us around Washington, D.C. We saw several of the Smithsonian museums. I had not realized until then that the institution was not housed in one building. We were not there long enough to visit all of them but we did see several of the exhibits that were housed in different buildings. We got to travel by the Metro train system. When they moved to Tulsa, Oklahoma, we visited there also.

Karen moved to Chicago and we visited there several times, visiting several areas that seemed really interesting. One of her apartments was near the lake, and one cold winter day I picked up rocks at the edge of the lake. Most of them were actually pieces of glass that had been tumbled smooth by the wave action of the water.

At that same apartment we got to see creativity in action. It was a very small place, probably intended for one person. But Karen had divided it using handmade bookcases to make bedrooms for three

A Good While Back

girls. She used full sheets of plywood, long side down, for the back of the bookcases and other boards for the ends and shelves. They really looked special.

We didn't get to visit John while he was living in California or Texas. I guess his jobs were not as permanent there, anyway.

Celia married and lived in Indiana for a while. Her first son was born in Indiana and we visited them there. Later her husband went into the military and they lived in Georgia. We visited her there, especially when she had babies. The army base was near Savanna and we got to see that pretty place.

On one outing we drove down into Florida to see some of that state and to see the ocean. We had taken little Samuel with us, and when he needed a restroom, not only did we not find a place to stop, we did not find a place to turn around and head back. When we finally got back to their housing he shot out of the car.

We also visited Celia and her family in San Antonio, Texas and later in Tuscon, Arizona. San Antonio had special places to see and we visited her there at least twice.

We had never ridden on a train until our visit to Tuscon. The reclining seats and footrests were a joke and of very little help for overnight travel. At San Antonio our passenger train waited overnight on a siding for a freight train—whose company owned the tracks—to pass through on those tracks. When we started the next morning a different engine was attached to the opposite end of the train and we traveled the rest of the way backwards to Tuscon.

When it was time for us to head home, the kids flew us back. There were also interesting things about that flight but that is another story.

In 1991, we learned my brother, Don, was dying of brain cancer. We flew out to see him in California, near Los Angeles. We had a nice visit and he died about a month later. He had lived about three months after his original diagnosis.

Chapter 13

When I start feeling sad that Ken is not here with me and see some of the many pictures he took, I have to remind myself we had some really good and special years.

My health has not improved with the years. After Ken passed I fell four times so I started using a Rollator. I fell once with the Rollator when I was careless and got knocked down by a heavy door. My legs are getting weaker but by being careful, and with help from the kids, I can do most of the things I want/need to do. I am now having weaker spells so that will probably be even more limiting but I am doing fairly well.

Our family has been having yearly reunions on July 4 since about 2001. We have spent several different years at Todd Hall Center just out of town for that holiday. It is an Episcopalian retreat, but some of the girls knew the Todd daughter so our family has been able to rent the old family house and some of the extra housing so we could all fit. At some point after Ken died, we started having our reunions at the house.

Samuel (grandson) and Stephanie had their large, beautiful wedding. I did not feel strong enough to travel to Austin, but I received plenty of pictures. The part of the family that was able to be there looked special and enjoyed their trip. A couple years later, Aria arrived, my first great granddaughter. They have come to visit me a couple times since she was born and I get to see lots of pictures on Facebook.

Time marches on. I decided that the trip to Westview Baptist Church in Belleville was too much for me to drive alone, even after being there for forty-five years or so.

After checking out the Columbia church and deciding I would have trouble with their stairs I had been going to the First Baptist Church in Waterloo for three years or so when I decided that drive was too much, too, and visited the First Baptist Church in Columbia.

The Columbia Church had built and moved into a new church building, leaving behind the old building at the location on Bottom Avenue.

When I visited the older ladies Sunday School Class I was a little surprised to be introduced with the addendum, "Her husband was a photographer." Several people remembered Ken that way.

Chapter 14

Notes and comments in preparing for Ken's funeral:

Kenisms:
Oy! Oy! (Oui, oui, monsieur.) This was to tease a friend who was a French language teacher.
Goose grease (good grief)
Horse-divers (for hors d'oeuvres)
Pie are not square, pie are round!
"Hey George!" (or Harry) When he was acting like he couldn't remember a kid's name.

Memories of the life of Kenneth Edwards (from his funeral):

How do you characterize a full life in just a few words?
Ken Edwards, our Dad, lived eighty-two years, was married to the love of his life for sixty-three years, helped raise six children, lived to see an extended set of nine grandchildren. He loved the family he grew up with: his parents, his brother and sister, who have gone on before him, his many cousins, aunts and uncles and his church family. He loved the family God gave him in his adult years, and we loved him. His quiet, steady wisdom was the air we breathed.
Dad and Mom were in complete accord in their core values, which they lived out with those around them and passed on to us,

their children. Dad treated others the way he wished to be treated; he passed on to us the Golden Rule. He worked hard, loved life, and endured with patience even those things that were not so pleasant. He endured the pain of failing health for a number of years, and even that endurance is a good model to follow.

The photos on display represent a small percentage of the family albums since most of the time Dad was behind the camera. In the last few days, going through all the pictures, we have relived many family events and magnificent out-of-doors images that Dad preserved for us.

Penni's first grade description of Dad for a school paper was that he led the singing at church and told jokes.

We remember those occasions when he would bring Lifesavers home in his lunch box for us. Chocolate was Celia's favorite and butter-rum was Penni's favorite.

One Christmas Dad made a barn for the boys, a dollhouse for Karen, and a dressing table for Penni.

Dad hung a rope swing in one of the trees in the backyard, which also became the climbing tree for the kids. He made stilts for Jeff and John one year. Another year he made a skating rink at the bottom of the hill, and much work was done to terrace the other side of the hill, purchased soon after, for the huge garden he and Mom tilled, planted, and harvested, with occasional weed-pulling or watering by the kids.

He loved to read, authors like Louis L'Amour, Dick Francis, Tom Clancy, and Zane Gray, and the *National Geographic* magazine. The last book he was reading/rereading was *Airport* by Arthur Haley. Had ordered *Reader's Digest* Condensed Books for many years. Spent many hours in his special library, which he designed with double bay windows and which Mom always called "his hidey-hole." He kept everything very orderly and organized, becoming even more intent on this in recent times. He also read his Bible every day for the last several years.

He enjoyed taking pictures, collecting cameras, working in his own darkroom. He'd had his own darkroom since he was a young teenager. His darkroom and woodshop were places to go when he needed to get away from six noisy kids. We could often hear him whistling as he worked—in particular "You Are My Sunshine"—whistled with a little bounce in the rhythm that was all his own.

He also entertained us by playing the harmonica, which acquired a few baby bite marks along the way. (Celia remembers testing the feel of metal on her teeth…she should have claimed to be learning to play it.) He liked to read airplane magazines such as *Sport Aviation* and went to many homebuilt airplane conventions and tried to keep up with them over the years.

He grew up in the country and had a special attachment to the land. He always had a garden of some sort. Even the last few years after moving to a place with a smaller yard he had a container garden.

When we were children attending the First Baptist Church in Columbia, Dad was the song leader, and we could be found every week (three times a week) sitting in the second pew where we could watch him. He was a deacon there, too, but what we remember more was his service as the church custodian. During that time we kids often helped him on Saturdays. Not saying for sure, but sometimes we kids may have scooted down the pews to hurry up the dusting of them.

There were many trips to Salem, Missouri, and when we got to the hilly country roads we would yell, "Faster, Dad, faster!" And he would! Our own roller coaster. Some of us liked that more than others did. Going to the Doss Store near the Pleasant Valley Baptist Church was a special treat, where each of us could choose one candy bar and one soda. Some of us would sit on spinning stools, and some on bales of hay, and might later need to visit the scary outhouse.

Mom talks about Dad with great love and will miss his calming influence and ability to coax a smile out of her even when she didn't feel like it. Penni remembers Dad holding Mom when she was crying because she was worried where the twenty-five dollars was coming from to pay for Celia to have the cut on her chin sutured at the doctor's office, and Dad reassuring Mom it would be okay. We all remember the kiss at the front door every day when Dad got home from work. Dad did not like being bossed around, but he would do almost anything if asked. Mom will miss the comfortable sharing of tasks such as Dad taking care of the technical gadgets, changing the light bulbs, making the coffee and stomping the recycle cans and boxes. She will miss the shared activities they had for over sixty-three years. She will miss her best friend and the love of her life.

It is hard to do justice in a short time to the memory of a life that was well lived. Dad loved his family and friends, and lived humbly before God and man. He did his very best to model a character of love and compassion, gentleness and self-control, endurance and faith in the Lord of his life. Dad understood that God is in control and has planned an eternity for us to be with Him. We look forward to the reunion when we will join him, but for now, we will all miss him.

Chapter 15

February 21, 2013

To Ken

You were here and now you are gone,
You left me here to carry on
    And I will.
I know you tried your very best
To just keep going. I am blessed.
    Though you were ill.

The doctors said your heart was fine.
I am not sure what they had in mind,
    But you had a will.
We were blessed as two. It is hard as one.
I have to do what you would have done.
    But I love you still.

A Good While Back

March 24, 2013

He Is Gone

I know that he is gone
For his bed is empty now.
It really is so very sad,
But I'll get by somehow.

The very best that I can do
Is to honor him somehow.
And not to change as I'm alone
Or too much grief allow.

He really tried to stay around
He pushed and did his best.
He did his usual family things
As if it were a test.

He bought the food and got the mail.
He did his very best.
He really tried to carry on.
He now deserves his rest.

April 11, 2013

Remember Me

Do not forget me was a refrain
That simmered and smoldered there in my brain.
    I know where it started.
    I know why it stayed.
It was like a mantra to forever be played.
It was as if after all that we had
That I might forget that he was Big Dad.

For more than sixty-three years,
Which was most of my life,
First and forever I was his wife.
    We were friends, we were lovers
    And we worked together.
We were a team in all kinds of weather.
Now that it's over, out it all shakes
That is just what is needed, just what it takes.

So no, I'll not forget the fun, trials too.
Though the world keeps going round.
I'll not forget you.

A Good While Back

May 22, 2013

What Is Real

This thing we call life,
Is it all just a dream,
With things not exactly
All that they seem?
Was I really someone's
Sweetheart, somebody's wife
Or was it just a dream
In this thing we call life?
Is the grass really green?
Are daffodils yellow?
Do babies grow up and old,
And wrinkled too?
Or is it really just people
Like me and like you?
I guess we will know
When it's all said and done,
The mystery of things
When this journey is done.

June 26, 2013

He Left

I can just imagine
As Ken started to leave
He thought of my welfare
Knew that I'd grieve.

But the angel said come.
It is your time to go.
We'll take care of her
In this world here below.

God gave her a brain,
You left an example.
Your life here below
Is just simply a sample
Of the love you will find
When you see Jesus
And the others you know
Who will be there to greet us.

The air is so rare
And the streets are of gold
And the sight that is heaven
Is a thing to behold.
So enjoy it my friend
She'll be along soon enough.
She'll do fine with our help.
She is made of stern stuff.

A Good While Back

Gifts

Finished September 17, 2013

I saw the moon and I thought of you
For it was something we used to do.
As you closed the drapes you would call to me.
So what you saw you could have me see.

The moon could be full or half or crescent,
But to us it was like a present,
Or clouds in the sky that were different or odd,
Were like a gift sent directly from God.

The gifts around us though large or small,
Were to us a clarion call
To worship the King and know that He cares
For we see all around us the things He shares.

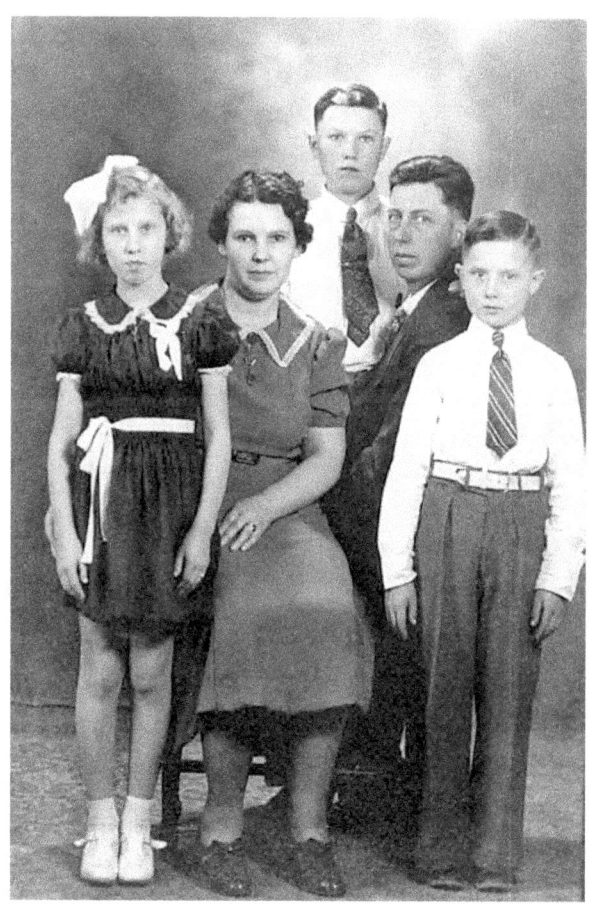

Naomia, Daphnia, Wilbur, Carl, Kenneth
Edwards

A Good While Back

Olieta and Kenneth

Keneth and Olieta's 50th Anniversary

Front: Olieta and Kenneth
Middle: Karen, Penni, Celia, Darla
Back: John, Jeff

www.ingramcontent.com/pod-product-compliance
Lightning Source LLC
Chambersburg PA
CBHW062208080426
42734CB00010B/1839